WINNING BACK THE WORDS

DATE DUE

WINNING BACK THE WORDS

Confronting Experts in an Environmental Public Hearing

Mary Richardson, Joan Sherman,
and Michael Gismondi

GARAMOND PRESS

A publication of Garamond Press

Garamond Press
Suite 403
77 Mowat Avenue
Toronto, Ontario
M6K 3E3

Cover photographs
Front cover: Mill-site resident Betty Sewall speaking at a hearing held in a local community hall. (Courtesy of *The Athabasca Advocate*)
Back cover: Athabasca, April 1, 1990 (Courtesy of *The Athabasca Advocate*)

Printed and bound in Canada

Canadian Cataloguing in Publication Data

Richardson, Mary
        Winning back the words: confronting experts in an
environmental public hearing

ISBN 0–920059–17–1

1. Investigations – Citizen participation.
2. Environmental impact analysis – Citizen participation.
3. Wood-pulp industry – Environmental aspects – Alberta –
Athabasca – Case studies.
I. Sherman, Joan. II. Gismondi, Michael Anthony. III. Title.

TD194.6.R5 1993   363.7   C93–094463–1

The Publishers acknowledge the financial support of the Canadian Studies and Special Projects Directorate of the Department of the Secretary of State, Government of Canada.

Contents

Acknowledgements

We would like to acknowledge the assistance of the people whose help made this book possible. Thanks to Louis Schmittroth and W. A. (Bill) Fuller who shelved the idea of retirement to work full time for a better environment; to the Friends of the Athabasca Environmental Association—if it weren't for them, we wouldn't have had these hearings; to all the people who spoke at the hearings—their participation inspired us to write this book. We regret that we could not include more of the contributions made by intervenors, in particular, Louis Schmittroth's important presentations on river modeling and dissolved oxygen. Peter Saunders of Garamond Press has been an enthusiastic supporter and encouraged us to tell this Canadian story. Thomas Dunk and Eric Higgs read the early manuscript and offered critical comments which we have tried to incorporate. Vince Foster, Les Cheshire, and Gloria Zahara prepared the graphics for the book. Special thanks to our friend and editor Gilda Sanders for her energy and good sense. We are grateful to Athabasca University for providing assistance so that the book could be printed in an environmentally responsible manner. Portions of the research on which this book is based were funded by Canadian International Development Agency's Canada-Asia Partnership, Social Sciences and Humanities Research Council of Canada, and Academic Research Committee of Athabasca University.

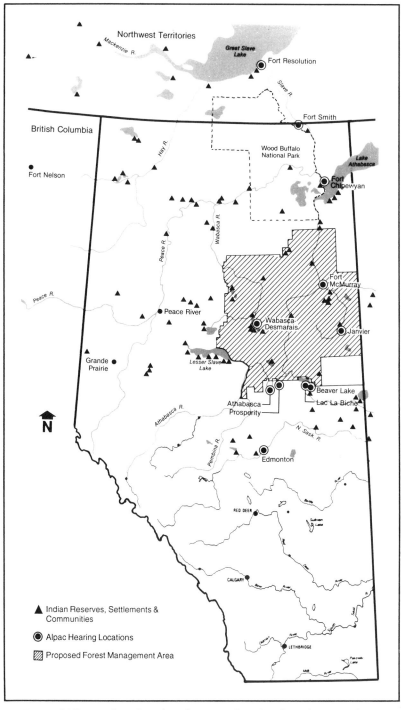

Map of Alberta showing the Alpac EIA hearing locations, native
communities, and the Alpac Forest Management Area (FMA)

Introduction

Six pulp and paper projects have come on-site before we, as members of the public, have had any input, and we have been shorn like the proverbial sheep. Now at last we are having hearings at which we can bleat. This possibility of being heard is a novelty, and it may well be the most important aspect of these hearings. Having an opportunity to stand up and speak out is a significant achievement, and, hopefully, this set of hearings will serve as a precedent for the examination of all public issues. And, just as the hearings conducted by Justice Thomas Berger on the need for the Mackenzie Pipeline set an example at the Federal level, so should these hearings on the desirability of another pulp mill on the Athabasca River serve as an example of what should in the future be done when important policy issues come up at the provincial level. . . . Such public hearings provide the only opportunity for minority groups to have their positions brought into the public domain. They are essential protection against the tyranny of the majority, and they should become mandatory adjuncts in the democratic process of informed decision-making. (Harry Garfinkle for the Green Party of Canada, Filed Document O-111:1)[1]

The public hearings that Harry Garfinkle talks about in the quotation above were the environmental impact assessment hearings for the Alberta-Pacific bleached kraft pulp mill, held in Alberta and the Northwest Territories in 1989-1990. This book introduces the reader to some of the people who had the strength and conviction to stand up and speak out at the hearings. Although some people spoke in favour of the mill, many challenged the claims of the proponent and the government that the mill would be environmentally sound, and would benefit them and their region of the province. In raising concerns and objections, those who opposed the mill challenged the combined forces of government and industry, and questioned widely held assumptions about the authority of experts.

Unlike abstract treatments of the structure and merits of public hearings, this book attempts to bring readers inside the Alberta-Pacific environmental hearing process, and to let them feel what it was like to participate. One objective of the book is to present concrete examples of how Canadians—farmers, trappers, truck drivers, students, natives, politicians, scientists, and entrepreneurs—spoke about the environment, economics, and democracy. Using quotations from hearing transcripts, the book recovers the voices of the people involved, and gives an impression of how complex the hearings were. People spoke not only to express their opinions about the project and its effects on the environment, but also to challenge the review process, to cross-examine pulp-mill executives, to question company experts and government specialists, and to take issue with the point of view of their neighbours. The book examines the language and other techniques used by proponents and opponents of the mill in their struggles to influence decision makers. We recognize the immense resources at the disposal of government and industry to convince the public to accept the project, but argue that members of the public did influence the outcome of the review. Finally, the book as a whole is a demonstration of the importance of participating in such political struggles.

Background

> In August 1988 . . . we began to hear rumors about a pulp mill; first we heard it might be a kraft mill, then we heard it would be the world's biggest. Then we had guys skulking around trying to get options on land and finally we had an announcement that in fact we would get all these things. Absolutely without public input. Well, not quite absolutely—the Chamber of Commerce, the Town Council, and the County Council were privy to all these plans, but the great Alberta public was not. [2]

If members of the public generally indicated a distrust of the proponent, they did not show any greater confidence in governments. The Alberta Government, in particular, was seen as approving the proposed mill without any credible public involvement, where the public could provide input upon which the decision would be based. The feeling was that only public pressure had forced the government to hold hearings. (Review Board Report)[3]

In December 1988, the premier of Alberta announced that Alberta-Pacific Forest Industries (Alpac) had been given approval in principle to build the world's largest single-line bleached kraft pulp mill along the Athabasca River, in the small farming community of Prosperity in Athabasca county, Alberta, Canada. At a cost of $1.3 billion, the Japanese-controlled mill would produce pulp from logs drawn from a wood supply area of 73,000 square kilometres of boreal mixed-wood forest (or 12 per cent of the Province of Alberta, an area approximately the size of New Brunswick).

The Alpac proposal brought to seven the number of pulp mills on the Peace-Athabasca watershed—two older kraft mills at Hinton and Grande Prairie, one kraft mill recently constructed at Peace River, two chemi-thermo-mechanical mills at Whitecourt and another at Slave Lake, and the proposed Alpac mill near Athabasca.

Environment Canada figures indicate that:

[T]he Pulp and Paper industry produces 50 per cent of all waste dumped into the nation's waters, and 80 per cent of all biological waste requiring oxygen for degradation— stripping oxygen from receiving waters, suffocating and killing aquatic life.[4]

As well, pulp mills that bleach with chlorine are responsible for releasing a large number of chlorinated organic compounds, including toxic dioxin and furan, which are persistent in the environment and bio-magnify up the food chain. At the time of the hearings, it was expected that Alpac alone would add some 1500 kilograms of organochlorines each day to the Athabasca River, bringing to five tonnes per day the total amount of organochlorines flowing into the feed waters of the Peace-Athabasca delta. The Peace and Athabasca rivers flow into Lake Athabasca, through the

Slave River into Great Slave Lake, down the Mackenzie River and eventually into the Arctic Ocean.

With a sense of urgency, the public tried to compel a comprehensive environmental impact assessment (EIA) of the Alpac project. Albertans raised a series of concerns: the rapidity with which the province was committing the north to forestry development (often by foreign-controlled transnational corporations) without public discussion of alternatives; the decision to site the mill in a farming community; and the shortcomings of a review process that excluded logging impacts from environmental impact assessment. Downstream native communities and the Government of the Northwest Territories also pressured the federal government to review the Alpac proposal because of potential negative health effects on native Canadians from eating fish contaminated with dioxin and furan from pulp-mill effluent.

The provincial government conducted a partial environmental impact assessment on the Alpac proposal in May 1989. Following Alberta guidelines, the company was required to develop an EIA document outlining the effects of its project on air, water, soil, and communities. Alpac then released the document for public review, and held public meetings in communities near the mill site in the spring and summer of 1989.[5] In Athabasca, participants were allowed ten minutes each to address the Alpac panel of experts and company bureaucrats. This initial review was intended, by both the Alberta government and the proponent, to constitute the public review aspect of the EIA.

However, when Alpac was unable to address many questions raised by environmentalists and civil servants, rising public pressure and the threat of litigation following the Federal Court decision on the Rafferty-Alameda Dam[6] compelled the federal and provincial governments to constitute the Alberta-Pacific EIA Review Board. Thus, the Province of Alberta was "dragged" into what was reputed to be the most comprehensive scrutiny of a pulp mill ever conducted in Canada.

The Alpac EIA Review Board represented various constituencies. Its members included four provincial government appointees (a local farmer; a local airline owner; the local school superintendent; the Chief of the Fort McKay Indian Band);[7] a representative of the Government of the Northwest Territories; and two federally appointed scientists (an internationally respected water quality researcher and a professor of environmental science with experience in EIA procedures). The Chairman was the head of the Energy Resources Conservation Board of Alberta.

Significantly, public pressure also led to a broadening of the terms of reference of the Review Board to include an examination of "the cumulative effects on the Peace-Athabasca river system of existing discharges as well as those which would result from the Alberta-Pacific and other proposed mills."[8] Forestry impacts, except as logging affected Indian Reserve lands, were excluded from review.[9] Public hearings on the Alpac pulp mill were held throughout northern Alberta and the Northwest Territories. Public pressure also forced the government to increase the number of hearing locations, from five to eleven, including the City of Edmonton. Testimony from 750 individuals, in the form of transcripts of oral presentations or written submissions to the Review Board, comprise more than 7000 pages.

In March 1990, the Alpac EIA Review Board released its report. The major recommendation of the Board was that the mill not be built until further studies showed that it would not pose a hazard to the river and to downstream users. The provincial government first agreed to abide by the Review Board's recommendation, but overturned its own decision nine months later. The mill is expected to begin operations in September 1993.

About the Book

This book reconstructs debates about several important issues that were raised at the hearings, using transcripts from the hearings, written submissions to the Review Board, letters and articles from newspapers, interviews with participants, personal correspondence, and the proponent's documentation. Each speaker at the hearings is identified by name, hearing location, and transcript page number or filed document number, so that the reader can get a sense of place and time within the hearings, and of how comments made at one hearing site might have been referred to or answered on a different day at another hearing location.

The book is organized into eight chapters. It opens with a chapter on the use of discourse analysis to examine struggles over power and control in public hearings. While much of the theoretical work on environmental public hearings is written in response to other theories, ours is also based on the experience of having participated in public hearings. From our experience, we argue that people can subvert the authority of expert or dominant discourses and break the constraints of the hearing process. Chapter 2 shows how the public reacted to the power structure of the Alpac hearings and avoided becoming hostage to the process. Chapter 3 examines the claim by the government and Alpac that this pulp mill would be an example of sustainable development, and recounts how the public resisted the restrictive conventions and influential discourses of economic development.

The next three chapters share a common theme: public questioning of the authority of scientists and experts. In Chapter 4, members of the public examine whether impact science is good science, and identify the value dimension of scientific findings reported in the EIA. In Chapter 5, ethnocentrism in health standards for consumption of fish contaminated with dioxins and furans is exposed. In Chapter 6, we move to the farming community proposed as the site for the mill. We show how local people disputed some of the assumptions and findings of the proponent and the government concerning impacts on their rural life.

From science and authority, we shift in Chapter 7 to the public's challenge to government and corporate ways of portraying the trade-off between jobs and the environment. Finally, Chapter 8 reveals the outcome of the first hearings, and discusses the scientific workshop on technical issues in which politicians and corporate interest groups overturned an environmentally oriented decision that had substantial public support. In the conclusion, we offer some thoughts from the trenches on the merits of participation in public hearings.

About the Authors

As members of the Friends of the Athabasca Environmental Association (FOTA), the authors fought for public hearings on the Alpac project, attended the hearings, spoke at them, submitted briefs, and questioned government and industry representatives. As the authors themselves participated, they are sometimes quoted as speakers at the hearings. The authors live and work in the Athabasca area.

Notes
1. All items identified in this work as "Filed Documents" are written submissions to the Alpac EIA Review Board, a collection of the Filed Documents is housed in the Athabasca University Library; quotations

from the Alberta-Pacific EIA Review Board public hearings cited in this volume are from J. G. Moore and Associates Ltd., *The Alberta-Pacific Environment Impact Assessment Review Board Public Hearing Proceedings, Volumes 1-55* (Edmonton, Alberta: J. G. Moore and Associates Ltd., 1989).

2. Bill Fuller, "Facing the Future—An Environmentalist's Perspective," in Kim Sanderson, ed., *Sustainable Use of Canada's Forests: Are We on the Right Path?* (Edmonton, Alberta: Canadian Society of Environmental Biologists, 1991), pp. 13-16. Quotation from p. 13.

3. Alberta-Pacific Environmental Impact Assessment Review Board, *The Proposed Alberta-Pacific Pulp Mill: Report of the Review Board March, 1990* (Edmonton, Alberta: Alberta Environment, 1990), p. 74.

4. Jessica Campbell, "Forum File: Index on Pulp and Paper Pollution," *Canadian Forum* (June/July 1991): 32.

5. The Government of Alberta promised public involvement and public input in reviewing the proposal. Alpac offered communities open houses, where people could meet one-on-one with company officials to learn about the project and to express their concerns. The public found this format unacceptable. At an open house in the downwind community of Lac La Biche, an angry crowd demanded a town hall meeting and a heated question and answer session involving some 200 community members followed. The debate at such meetings served to educate locals about the breadth of shared concerns, and to identify and publicize shortcomings in the development proposal.

6. The Federal Court ruled in 1989 that the federal government had to conduct a full EIA on the Rafferty and Alameda dam projects in Saskatchewan. This decision set a precedent for other large projects which would affect areas of federal responsibility, such as inter-boundary waters. In the case of the Alpac project, the federal and provincial governments decided to conduct a joint review to avoid duplication.

7. Three members or alternates initially appointed to the Review Board resigned because of conflict of interest. For example, the selection of a local General Motors dealer to the board backfired when Friends of the Athabasca produced a newspaper advertisement he had purchased that declared his business's support for the Alpac proposal.

8. Alberta-Pacific Environmental Impact Assessment Review Board, p. 5.

9. In Canada, Indian Reserve lands are a federal responsibility, as are migratory birds, inter-boundary waters, fisheries and oceans and national parks—all of which were relevant to the Alpac proposal. Forestry is under provincial jurisdiction, and is jealously guarded by Alberta's Ministry of Forestry, Lands and Wildlife. The Minister refused to allow his wildlife and public lands staff to participate in the Alpac hearings.

Three of the Alpac EIA Review Board Members
(Photograph courtesy of *The Athabasca Advocate*)

CHAPTER 1

Discourse and Counter-discourse in Environmental Public Hearings

[T]he objective of a public hearing process is not to destroy or sabotage a proposal. Neither is it to muzzle criticism of that proposal; nor is the hearing a forum for an initiator to promote a proposal. Ideally, a hearing should provide an opportunity for a dynamic exchange of views leading to conclusions that make it possible to improve a proposal that is compatible with the environment or to reject a proposal that constitutes a threat to the quality of the natural or social environment. (Study Group on Environmental Assessment Hearing Procedures)[1]

Our starting point in this book is a statement by the Study Group on Environmental Assessment Hearing Procedures outlining the purpose of environmental public hearings. The authors of the report, *Public Review: Neither Judicial, Nor Political, But an Essential Forum for the Future of the Environment,* champion public hearings as "a service requested of the public by the government to help it make an informed decision and to favor a harmonious relationship between economic development and environmental protection." For these researchers, the public hearing serves as a means of defining "the values which the population associates with a specific proposal" and as "a forum in which expert opinions on technical subjects as well as value judgments or the choices of society may intersect and merge."[2]

The Group's position is based on many assumptions, one of which is that the role of the public at an environmental public hearing is to make value judgements or choices about a development, and that the proper role of experts is to state the facts about the development and predict its effects on the environment. Behind this assumption, in turn, is the further assumption that there is a clear separation between facts and values, so that it is possible for technical experts to confine themselves to the facts, that is, to be as objective as possible, and not to stray into the area of values. The statement further assumes that technical experts are the people best qualified to determine the environmental effects of large-scale industrial projects, although the Group argues that the public can identify issues that might not have been considered by the proponent, and can provide knowledge of the local area.[3] Finally, the title of the report indicates that the Study Group believes that environmental public hearings can be non-political, in the sense that their outcomes will be unaffected by questions of power, and will be based on fact and public choice alone. The Group sees no power imbalance between the public and the technical experts, or between the public and the proponent. Each party is an equal partner in the process, and if each party does its part, a decision will be arrived at that benefits both the economy and the environment.

Each of these assumptions is questionable, and all were questioned by participants of the Alpac public hearings. To a large extent, it was Alpac's use of the hearing process to "muzzle criticism" and "promote its proposal" that spurred participants to intensify their questioning of the project and to criticize aspects of the Alpac hearing process itself.

In this study, we engage in discourse analysis to show how language was used in the Alpac hearings in an attempt to gain, consolidate, and maintain power. This chapter explains why discourse analysis is a good tool for understanding the dynamics, and debating the efficacy, of a public hearing.

Language and Power

All day long here I've been trying to do a little translation going both ways, but I can't help it if I'm more or less biased towards my people because . . . after all, I'm an Indian person and I think like an Indian person. I have an education also, but I didn't let that lead me astray. . . . I'll interpret to you what I said here earlier. Maybe that's what somebody didn't like, the way I interpreted it. What I said [in translating what Alpac had said to the elders] was, these people here that Alpac hires, they get paid by Alpac. So

more or less, they are going to tend to lean towards saying
what Alpac is paying them to say. That's what I was telling
my leaders here. It's just like me. I'm an Indian person. I'm
going to lean towards promoting an Indian point of view.
(Ron Lameman, Beaver Lake: 1314)[4]

There is an inherent power imbalance between project proponents and members of the public in an environmental public
hearing. Before a project gets to the stage at which a public hearing
will be held, the proponent must have committed a great deal of
money to the project, and secured backing from the government. In
the case of the Alpac proposal, the Alberta government that set up
the public hearings was the very government that had already given
approval in principle to the project, and had agreed to issue
debentures and provide financial support for infrastructure.

Many members of the public and researchers in the field of
environmental studies think that the public hearing is so tightly
controlled by the powerful interests of the proponent and the
government that members of the public who object to the project
cannot make their concerns heard, let alone be taken seriously. One
example that reinforces this belief is the way the provincial government, co-sponsor of the Alpac review, succeeded in preventing the
effects of forestry operations from being considered as part of the
environmental impact assessment. Speaker after speaker at the
public hearings objected to this narrowing of the terms of reference
of the EIA, but no serious debate was allowed to take place.

Limiting the terms of reference of a public hearing over the
objections of the public is an obvious exercise of power, and as
such, is dangerous for the government. There are other, more subtle
ways that governments and project proponents can limit debate
and legitimate the desired outcome of the hearing, including dress,
demeanour, and a choice of words intended to indicate expertise,
trustworthiness, objectivity, and concern for the well-being of
society. These techniques are simultaneously used to marginalize
and dismiss concerns raised by anyone who questions or objects to
the proposal. For example, large industrial projects are called
"developments" by their proponents. As development has positive
connotations for most people, and is described in terms that make
it appear natural and necessary for economic well-being, it is hard
from the outset to raise serious questions about alternatives, or to
ask whether a project will deliver on its economic promises. It is

especially hard to raise these questions when the project is backed by a respected provincial government. Thus, the difficulty is not so much whether the public can speak at a public hearing—that, after all, is what public hearings are for—but if questions and objections can be ignored as irrelevant or brushed aside, we must ask instead whether the public can be heard—and taken seriously.

In *The Power and the Word: Language, Power and Change*, Roger Anderson argues that "behind many of the variations in language use lie differences in social power," and that "social power can be created and justified through discourse and practices shaped by language." Thus, if we are interested in understanding how decisions about industrial projects are made, "we must concentrate more on the variations in language and how they relate to actual users in specific situations."[5] In subsequent chapters we examine how identifiable groups or individuals used words, such as "sustainable development" or "leading-edge technology," to affect the outcome of the Alpac public hearings.

How can language be used to influence the outcome of a public hearing, in a way that allows the hearing process to appear open, and not an arbitrary exercise of power? In *Discourse and the Construction of Society*, Bruce Lincoln distinguishes between force and discourse, and explains the power and the ideological effects of discourse:

> Discourse supplements force in several important ways, among the most important of which is ideological persuasion. In the hands of elites and of those professionals who serve them (either in mediated fashion or directly), discourse of all forms—not only verbal, but also the symbolic discourses of spectacle, gesture, costume, edifice, icon, musical performance, and the like—may be strategically employed to mystify the inevitable inequities of any social order and to win consent of those over whom power is exercised, thereby obviating the need for the direct use of coercive force and transforming simple power into "legitimate" authority.[6]

Michel Foucault explains the effect of discourse in a similar way when he says that it is not a repressive but a "permissive" way of exercising power.

> The exercise of power consists in guiding the possibility of conduct and putting in order the possible outcomes. . . . Basically power is less a confrontation between two adversaries or the linking of one to the other than a question of government. . . . To govern, in this sense, is to structure the possible field of action of others.[7]

Discourses can embody two kinds of governing techniques: the first are totalizing techniques that privilege and legitimate the knowledge, competence, and qualifications of one social group; the second are individualizing techniques, "a form of power that makes individuals into subjects." Drawing on an analysis of power relationships in the Christian practice of confession, Foucault calls the latter type of power "pastoral" power.

> [T]his form of power cannot be exercised without knowing the inside of people's minds, without exploring their souls, without making them reveal their innermost secrets. It implies a knowledge of the conscience and an ability to control it.[8]

For Foucault the modern state is a new organization with great pastoral power. It integrates the individual into the state "under one condition, that this individuality would be shaped in a new form and submitted to a set of very specific factors."[9]

Adam Ashforth[10] uses Foucault's analysis to criticize commissions of inquiry, such as Royal Commissions,[11] which are similar to environmental impact assessment review hearings. He shows that they do much more than "serve only the purposes they proclaim— of impartial fact-finding and advice." For him, public hearings are "symbolic rituals within modern States, theatres of power" that legitimate states and allow them to "sit above 'Society' as the embodiment of the 'common good'." Moreover, inquiries extend the knowledge and power of the state into the innermost consciousness and secret soul of social activists, including environmentalists, in ways that "make possible the work of organizing political subjection."[12] Ashforth believes that governments establish public hearings to placate the public by making people believe they have power that they do not have. Thus, if citizens take part in a public hearing believing that they can influence its outcome, they unwittingly participate in their own subjugation.

Ashforth's critique of commissions of inquiry is persuasive, and helps explain the frustration and feelings of powerlessness that many participants in the Alpac hearings said they experienced when trying to express their opinions. Not surprisingly, Alpac's pro-development discourses were designed to appeal to common sense and to deflect criticism of the project. Hence, when we examine the hearing transcripts, we are certainly concerned with the rhetorical power of dominant discourses, and with their power to distort reality or mask the proponent's efforts to present reality in a particular way. But we disagree with Ashforth's tendency to view the people who are "the public" as passive, unwitting victims of state and corporate manipulation. Our analysis identifies moments in the Alpac hearings when less-powerful groups undermined the discourses empowered by the dominant groups, and in the process, constructed counter-discourses.[13] Throughout the book, we will be highlighting both Alpac's rhetorical techniques and the attempts by its opponents to weaken the hold of the dominant discourse on the hearings.

We do not read these social or ideological confrontations in the same way that some literary critics would read the internal relationship of discourses in texts. The confrontations we witnessed were not lost or won simply on the battlefield of meanings. When individuals or organized groups undertake to question corporate, state, and scientific conventions, those individuals or groups must confront the ideological and social power of big business, the democratic state, and the scientific establishment. Subverting dominant discourses and asserting counter-discourses are political acts; in this case, they were acts motivated by concern for environmental protection, transformation of the political process, and participation and control at community levels.

Moreover, struggles over discourse occur in the midst of complex social and historical processes that affect the degree to which resistance is likely to be effective. To give a simple example, public opinion is important to the political culture of Canada, and must be taken into account by decision makers. Thus, resistance to the construction of a large-scale industrial project is more likely to be effective if there has been a disastrous accident, or a record of public concern about environmental pollution, in a similar industry in the recent past. For this reason, we must examine struggles in the Alpac hearings in the light of an institutional and social context in which concern for the environment was number one in the national opinion polls, and in which pulp mills were recognized as heavy polluters of fresh water lakes and rivers in Canada.

Environmental reviews often operate in complex institutional contexts which involve both the federal and provincial governments. There is a long history of provincial-federal conflict about jurisdiction over resource development in Alberta and other provinces. These conflicts have presented opportunities for resistance that have been exploited by pressure groups. One tactic has been to pit federal and provincial politicians and bureaucrats, and their differing regulatory obligations and standards, against one another. For example, in the late 1980s, provincial-federal power struggles over responsibility for environmental protection were fundamentally altered when the Federal Court forced a federal review of a Saskatchewan mega-project, the Rafferty-Alameda Dam, in mid-construction. This "was not the result of a federal power grab. Rather, at the behest of environmental groups, the courts thrust jurisdiction upon a reluctant federal government."[14] In the Alpac case, public pressure compelled federal representation on the Review Board, and the public review benefited, because interventions by federal scientists and technical experts helped to legitimate popular challenges to provincial and company experts.

Furthermore, debates about larger social and political issues, some of which extended beyond the national context, influenced the course of the hearings, and ensured that the results were not a foregone conclusion.[15] In the last few years, for example, there have been lively debates about the ability of native people to continue to pursue their traditional life-style (hunting and trapping), to govern themselves, and to assert control over resource development on their traditional land. Previously, the trapping issue had pitted environmentalists and native people against each other. However, when some native leaders publicly promoted the Alpac project, the threat to traditional life-styles, and to control of forest and wildlife resources, made possible alliances between traditional natives and environmentalists. Laurie Adkin notes, in "Counter-hegemony and Environmental Politics in Canada," that when counter-hegemonic discourses and alliances are formed, "the basic elements of discourse shift."[16] For example, debates that opposed trapping rights to wildlife protection gave way to a united call for protection of the boreal forest, its wildlife—flora and fauna—and the people who live in it. The groups in conflict and the labels applied to them also shifted. Instead of anti-Greenpeace natives *versus* animal-rights non-

native environmentalists, the opposition became those who supported Alpac's development project *versus* those who championed
the environmental protection that made traditional life-styles
possible.

Using Literary Tools in Social Analysis

> The real-life sense and significance of an utterance (of
> whatever kind it might be) does not coincide with the purely
> verbal components of the utterance. The spoken words are
> imbued with what is implied and unspoken.[17]

Song, poetry, humour, story-telling, life-history, and outrageous or
arresting metaphors were some of the tools people used to criticize
Alpac, to cross-examine its expert witnesses, and to draw attention
to how Alpac was presenting its case. This section outlines some of
the techniques used by anti-mill forces to break through authoritative discourses and to draw attention, as Bakhtin says,[18] to the
values, opinions, and sources of legitimation implied but unspoken
by mill proponents. In the following chapters, we examine how
these techniques were used in specific areas of disagreement.

Mariana Valverde identifies techniques from literary criticism
that are useful to critical social analysis and activism, including the
deconstruction of binary oppositions and the analysis of rhetorical
metaphors or tropes.[19] Binary oppositions, such as scientist *versus*
environmentalist or jobs *versus* the environment, are used to place
two things in a hierarchy, to ensure that one is favoured over the
other. The former opposition, for example, plays to the belief that
scientists deal objectively with facts, while environmentalists and
concerned citizens may be well-meaning, but deal with emotions
and values. This belief often leads to a discounting of what is said by
environmentalists or non-specialists. The latter opposition suggests
that you cannot make jobs by protecting the environment. Each
opposition works to undermine the credibility of one side and to
support that of the other. Such oppositions also exacerbate political
disagreements, rather than facilitating a search for common ground.

Oppositions were crucial to the debates about the Alpac proposal: expert *versus* non-expert; local people *versus* outsiders; new
technologies *versus* old technologies; standards in Alberta *versus*
those in the rest of Canada; community-minded citizens *versus*
complainers; nature as resource *versus* nature as having spiritual

value. Breaking through such dichotomies opens up environmental issues to broader scrutiny, not only of what is said, but also of what may have been closed off, implied, or left unsaid because of the opposition.

The second technique Valverde discusses is the analysis of figures of speech: "Discourse that aims at persuading an audience and generating social action is often structured not so much through formal logic but through tropes, most notably metaphors but including the whole range of techniques taught by the ancients."[20] In the Alpac hearings, such metaphors abound: trees were "weeds"; effluents were "contributions"; chlorine was "an element of table salt"; government financial subsidies were "commitments"; deforestation and pulp mills were "forest industry initiatives"; pulp mill design changes were "tools in place to achieve environmental harmony"; low amounts of toxins in effluent were "no observed effect"; logging was "harvesting"; clearcuts were "patchcuts"; and forests were "getting old and dying instead of being put to good use." Such expressions work to persuade the public that the forest is solely an economic resource, and that pulp mill development is desirable and can be achieved without significant pollution. Challenging such figures of speech, or displacing them with equally powerful counter-metaphors and tropes, became a political tactic of mill opponents.

Following Valverde's lead, we have identified other techniques Alpac proponents used, such as linking their claims about the project to beliefs deeply embedded in our culture: the impersonal authority of science and technology; the wisdom of the market; the need for job creation to keep the traditional rural family together; the superiority of humans over nature; the ability of technology to solve social problems. Gordon and Suzuki, in their book *It's a Matter of Survival*, label these discourses "sacred truths" and give as examples "pollution is the price of progress," "all of nature is at our disposal," "growth is progress," and "nature is infinite."[21] Because what is sacred is authoritative, and what is profane is not, struggles to break the shackles of these categorizations take on political importance.

The rhetorical techniques we have been discussing, such as appeal to sacred truths, were used singly, in combination with one another, and in combination with other techniques. In our analysis of scientific discourses, we show how even grammatical techniques, such as the use of the passive voice and of impersonal pronouns, were employed to enhance Alpac's case.

Subverting dominant tropes, hierarchies, and sacred truths was not easy, because often the members of the public who were making the challenge lacked the social authority to do so. When topics such as nature or community or science were discussed in the hearings, a series of struggles over identity arose. The issue became, who should be identified as speaking with authority for a community?—for science?—for nature?—for native people?—for the silent majority? —for future generations? It quickly became apparent that establishing authority to speak was a highly political and hotly contested act. The authority of many speakers was not fixed *a priori*, but constructed and established in the course of the hearings. Similarly, people resisted being identified with labels perceived to have negative connotations, such as "extremist."

An example from the Alpac hearings of a dispute over identity and authority was the disagreement over who was entitled to speak about their environmental concerns to the Alpac Review Board, and how much the concerns of certain identifiable groups should weigh. Many people around Athabasca felt that hearings should not be held in Edmonton, because the people there had nothing to do with the boreal forest, the river, or the mill. Alpac was an issue for northerners. They claimed that people identified as "outsiders" should have little say.[22] Urban residents countered that, because the forests were on crown, or public, land, they were entitled to speak, and that their concerns for the environment were of equal weight to concerns of people who lived near Athabasca. Edmontonians forced the government to hold additional hearings in their city. Likewise, people downstream from Athabasca (especially residents of northern native communities and the people of the Northwest Territories), felt that their very lives depended on their speaking, and being heard, at the hearings. In each case, speakers sought to establish their social identity, either to diminish the weight of another's testimony, or to augment the authority given to their own arguments and to promote their side of the debate over the other.

In summary, our work shows how language was used during the Alpac public hearings to solidify the authority of experts, bureaucrats and business people.[23] We also show how significant numbers of citizens demystified authority by rejecting certain characterizations of environmental impacts, certain categories of discussion that Alpac used in its EIA to frame and limit debate, and even the imposition of certain identities.

The Value of Public Hearings

> [C]itizen participation in the management of . . . resources
> has taken many forms over the years. But, without exception
> it seems, they have been little more than fraudulent deceits,
> designed to defuse protest, co-opt the public, and enable
> the government, later, to say that it consulted the people.[24]

Many theorists affirm the importance of public participation for revealing value conflicts and value diversity, and for making explicit issues and concerns that might not otherwise be considered by decision makers. Accounting for and accommodating non-economic values, determining divergence in scientific opinions, gauging public acceptance, providing a forum for communication among scientists, proponents, civil servants, communities and people— public hearings are designed "not only to give people a chance to be heard, but to enhance the quality of decision making."[25]

In "Ethics and Institutions," Ted Schrecker argues for openness and public participation in environmental decision making, because it provides opportunities for the public to scrutinize the values and priorities implicit in expert testimony and in decisions taken by governments. He holds that policy decisions on environmental issues cannot be made simply on the basis of scientific enquiry. For example, since decisions about large industrial projects must be made in the face of uncertainty about their environmental impacts, value judgements must be made about how much risk is acceptable.

> In Canada, these decisions are characterized by broad areas
> of unappealable administrative discretion, high levels of
> secrecy and few formal avenues of access to information
> and participation . . . . The effect is to facilitate the ca-
> mouflaging of important ethical conflicts as decisions about
> scientific evidence or commonsense weightings of costs and
> benefits, especially when that process of camouflaging
> serves the ends of powerful beneficiaries of the *status quo*.[26]

Schrecker advocates reform of the process of environmental regulation to correct the imbalance.

Others, who support public hearings in principle, regret that hearings occur only after development decisions have been made, relegating public participation to reactions to prior decisions.

Project-specific assessments do not allow for proper review and examination of the government policies that elicit development proposals in the first place. Even those who support hearings note with dismay that there are no requirements compelling government agencies to abide by the outcomes of the hearings.[27] Frank Tester finds the federal environmental assessment review process to be "largely directed by interested authorities and limited to an advisory function."

> In 36 cases that were subjected to public panel review between the inception of the process in 1973 and January 1992, consideration of the underlying development issues was consistently discouraged and most deliberations were focused on the mitigation of negative effects. . . . Thus while federal assessment reviews have provided a forum for citizen participation, they have not provided an opening for successful challenges to conventional "development" projects.[28]

Tester is encouraged, however, by efforts to reform the hearing process, and to extend public participation into public scrutiny of private sector operations.[29]

Those who object to hearings dislike public participation for diverse reasons. On one end of the spectrum are those business people who feel public hearings prolong an already tedious review process. They believe that hearings are better left to bureaucrats and technical experts. Alongside them are those who complain that hearings become soap boxes for the uninformed, the emotional, and the ideological—the "Stalins of greenery."[30] They fear that the members of a hearing panel may be overly influenced by an unqualified public. For example, at the height of the Alpac hearings, Alberta Public Works Minister, Ken Kowalski, complained that the hearings favoured small environmental groups over the silent majority who, he claimed, supported the pulp mills: "It is a truism of life, that you tend to be captured by single-interest groups in our democratic society." Kowalski lamented that the silent majority could end up suffering because of "delays, confusion, uncertainty and final cancellation of the project . . . the possibility will always exist that a project such as the Alpac project can be scuttled by self-interest groups."[31]

Some business commentators see the power of the market itself threatened when unnecessarily stringent environmental reviews, regulations, and guidelines for conservation are imposed on industrial development. A columnist for *The Globe and Mail* wrote that:

> [The] Alberta Government . . . created a monster regulatory legacy that could harm development for years to come. In effect, the province has turned over economic decision-making to roving bands of environmentalists, ecologists, preservationists, conservationists, bureaucrats, review boards, nationalists and a host of other pressure groups and pseudo-forestry and economic experts.[32]

At the other end of the spectrum are those who find the public hearing process ineffective for protecting the environment from government schemes and business interests. Ray Kemp studied a British nuclear inquiry which was similar to a Canadian public hearing. Looking closely at the speech context of the hearing process, he concluded that, "public inquiries . . . serve to legitimize the actions and interests of dominant groups . . . a primary mechanism through which this is achieved is the systematic distortion of the communication process."[33] Using Habermas's concept of the ideal speech situation, he argued that public hearings do not provide unconstrained conditions for rational exploration and weighing of issues. Participants in the nuclear hearings had neither financial assistance nor opportunities equal to those of the company and government experts to put questions and direct discussions, to speak freely without pressure and influence, to forbid certain arguments, and to criticize statements and explanations.

Brian Wynne draws similar conclusions about public inquiries. For him, they resemble rituals which can order and control the public because, as "people's goals and values are held to be often vague, conflicting, [and] unstable," public opinion is "open to persuasion" by experts and expert discourses. It is not blind faith in the hearing process that victimizes the public. Rather, the public falls victim to hearing process techniques: "language, including technical analysis, can tacitly guide people into seeing the world in certain ways, influencing what is regarded as an accepted value, and what is inevitable, possible, desirable, or at least tolerable."[34] The effects of language that Wynne discusses—value imposition, inevitability, tolerance, acceptance—are deterrents to criticism and agency, and obstacles to the mobilization of opposition to any development project.

Although rituals appear to be collective and consensual, participation in a ritual such as a public hearing is governed by practices, conventions, and ways of acting determined by authorities. Wynne notes that power can be exercised in a ritual because "ritual processes and utterances [i.e., symbolic actions] . . . affirm the effectiveness, objectivity, and trustworthiness of key institutions." Typically, in this age of science and technology, the scientific expert or professional specialist—such as an engineer—enjoys great trust and status at a public hearing. For Wynne, public hearings create in the public mind an acceptance that complex issues should be reserved "for expert analysis"[35] and are not something to be decided by the broader public.

One might conclude, on the basis of Kemp's and Wynne's analyses, that members of the public who participate in public hearings are either willing or unwitting dupes of the process. Either they try to make a difference in a situation that is hopelessly stacked against them, or they do not even realize the hearing is controlled to such an extent that dissent will not be registered.

Are participants dupes? Or is there some chance that they will have an effect on the hearing? The studies by Kemp and Wynne on hearings in Britain tend toward an ahistorical and static reading of both language and the ritual-like qualities of public hearings. Hence, they suggest that outcomes will always be the same. We side with those social historians and anthropologists who have shown that public rituals "can act both to reinforce order and to suggest alternatives to the existing order."[36] The outcome of a hearing process is more open-ended than Kemp and Wynne suggest, and is dependent on context and political struggle. Challenges can take various forms: struggles between experts, struggles between lay people and experts, struggles over who can speak with authority on a subject, struggles over the meanings of words and concepts, struggles over values. We see public argument as a kind of resistance, and we explore language in its social and historical context. In our review of the Alpac hearings, we have found many challenges to the trust that the public puts in experts and expert knowledge. We argue our case on the basis of what people said in the hearings, and on the Review Board's report.

Notes

1. Study Group on Environmental Assessment Hearing Procedures, *Public Review: Neither Judicial, Nor Political, But an Essential Forum for the Future of the Environment,* A Report Concerning the Reform of Public Hearing Procedures for Federal Environmental Assessment Reviews (Ottawa: Supply and Services Canada, 1988), pp. 2-3.
2. Study Group, pp. 1, 2, 12.
3. Study Group, p. 26.
4. All items identified as "Filed Documents" are written submissions to the Alpac EIA Review Board, a collection of the Filed Documents is housed in the Athabasca University Library; quotations from the Alberta-Pacific EIA Review Board public hearings are from J. G. Moore and Associates Ltd., *The Alberta-Pacific Environment Impact Assessment Review Board Public Hearing Proceedings, Volumes 1-55* (Edmonton, Alberta: J. G. Moore and Associates Ltd., 1989).
5. Roger Andersen, *The Power and the Word: Language, Power and Change* (London: Paladin Grafton Books, 1988), pp. 9, 285.
6. Bruce Lincoln, *Discourse and the Construction of Society: Comparative Studies of Myth, Ritual, and Classification* (New York: Oxford University Press, 1989), pp. 4-5.
7. Michel Foucault, "The Subject and Power," *Critical Inquiry* 8 (Summer 1982): 777-795. Quotation from pp. 789-790.
8. Michel Foucault, p. 783.
9. Michel Foucault, p. 783.
10. A. Ashforth, "Reckoning Schemes of Legitimation: On Commissions of Inquiry as Power/Knowledge Forms," *Journal of Historical Sociology* 3, no. 1 (March 1990): 1-22.
11. See V. Seymour Wilson, "The Role of Royal Commissions and Task Forces," in G. B. Doern and P. Aucoin, eds., *The Structures of Policy-making in Canada* (Toronto: MacMillan, 1971), pp. 113-129; P. Resnick, "State and Civil Society: The Limits of a Royal Commission," *Canadian Journal of Political Science* 20, no. 2 (June 1987): 379-401.
12. Adam Ashforth, pp. 1, 4, 12, 17.
13. See J. C. Scott, *Domination and the Arts of Resistance* (New Haven: Yale University Press, 1990). Scott develops the liberative possibilities of resistance. See also the critique of Foucault's work by P. Willis and P. Corrigan, "Orders of Experience: The Differences of Working-class Cultural Forms," *Social Text* 7 (Spring-Summer 1983): 85-103.
14. Kathyrn Harrison, "Federalism, Environmental Protection, and Blame Avoidance" (Paper delivered at the Canadian Political Science Association Annual Meeting, Kingston, Ontario, 1991), p. 18.
15. The context of the Alpac hearings included debates about the expansion of the global forest industry into previously unused hardwood resource areas; predictions of high prices for premium pulp; the globalization of markets; the Canada-US Free Trade Agreement; the Alberta government's open invitation to offshore companies, such as Mitsubishi, to develop the boreal forest; the personalities and political aspirations of the environment ministers; the paramilitary style of the forestry depart-

ment and its minister; and the Canadian constitutional negotiations. These issues were debated in a context of a growing global concern about environmental problems: the greenhouse effect; de-forestation; increasing evidence of dioxin and furan contamination from pulp mills in Canada; the closing of shellfish fisheries in British Columbia; and a rise in the membership of organized environmental and public advocacy groups. The local context included the recent move of Athabasca University to the small town of Athabasca; the residence of two retired scientists in the impact area; and the presence of a well-organized New Democratic Party Association in the riding where Alpac would build.

16. Laurie E. Adkin, "Counter-hegemony and Environmental Politics in Canada," in William K. Carroll, ed., *Organizing Dissent: Contemporary Social Movements in Theory and Practice* (Toronto: Garamond Press, 1992), pp. 135-156. Adkin defines counter-hegemony as "those discourses critical of capitalist accumulation, of productivism, of science as domination of nature, of the prevailing ideologies of science and technocracy, of relations of subordination-domination (gender, racial, heterosexual), and of the institutions and social practices which underpin such relations, including the restricted nature of liberal democracy and the separation of the personal from the political, or the private from the public." All quotations from p. 136.

17. Quoted in Ken Hirschkop, "Bakhtin, Discourse and Democracy," *New Left Review* 160 (November-December 1986): 92-113. Quotation from p. 95. The author quoted is V. N. Volashinov, "Discourse in Life and Discourse in Poetry" in *Bakhtin School Papers*, p. 17.

18. See Ken Hirschkop, pp. 92-113; Bryan Palmer, *Descent into Discourse: The Reification of Language and the Writing of Social History* (Philadelphia: Temple University Press, 1990).

19. Mariana Valverde, "As if Subjects Existed: Analysing Social Discourses," *Canadian Review of Sociology and Anthropology* 28, no. 2 (1991): 173-187. Valverde dismisses the simplistic use of literary techniques to analyse social discourses, but avoids the rejection of literary analysis by critics such as Bryan Palmer.

20. Mariana Valverde, p. 179.

21. Anita Gordon and David Suzuki, *It's a Matter of Survival* (Toronto: Stoddard, 1990), pp. 1, 53.

22. See Thomas Dunk, "Talking About Trees: Images of the Environment and Society in Forest Workers' Discourse" (Paper delivered at the sessions on "Sociology and the Environment," at the CSAA Annual meetings, Charlottetown, PEI June 1992). Dunk notes that the identity of forest workers is "often formed around a set of oppositions to real or imaged 'others' (such as environmentalists or forest service inspectors) . . . the expression of attitudes about 'others' is also . . . a way of constructing an identity, of creating social boundaries." Draft copy, p. 23.

23. See Pierre Bourdieu, *Language and Symbolic Power,* edited and with an introduction by John B. Thompson, translated by Gino Raymond and Matthew Adamson (Cambridge: Polity Press, 1991).

24. Jim Rutkowsky and Joel Russ, "Forests, Water and Public 'Participation'," *The New Catalyst*, no. 23 (Spring 1992): 4-5.

25. Paul Edwards, *The Al-Pac Review Hearings: A Case Study* (Edmonton, Alberta: The Environmental Law Centre, 1990), p. 28. See also Peter Jacobs and Barry Sadler, *Sustainable Development and Environmental Assessment: Perspectives on Planning for a Common Future* (Ottawa: Canadian Environmental Assessment Research Council, 1991); R. Parenteau, *Public Participation in Environmental Decision-making* (Hull, Quebec: Federal Government Assessment Review Office, 1988); Lynn Cover, "Solving the Paradox of Public Participation in Environmental Planning: Evaluation of an Alberta Case Study," (Major paper for Masters Diss., York University, 1992). Cover concludes that public participation is a paradox: it is considered essential, but it is ineffective.

26. Ted Schrecker, "Ethics and Institutions: How We Think About Policy Decisions," *Environmental Ethics,* R. Bradley and S. Duguid, eds. (Burnaby, BC: Institute for the Humanities, Simon Fraser University, 1989), pp. 207-215. Quotation from p. 211. See also Edwin Levy, "The Swedish Studies of Pesticides and Cancer: An Example of Mandated Science" in *Environmental Ethics,* pp. 187-200. Liora Salter defines "mandated science" as science used for the purposes of making public policy, in *Mandated Science: Science and Scientists in the Making of Standards* (Dordrecht, Holland: Kluwer Academic Publishers, 1988), p. 2.

27. See Lynn Cover, p. 6. In the Alpac case, it would have meant a review of the government's policy to diversify the economy into forest products and pulp and paper.

28. Frank Tester, "Reflections on Tin Wis: Environmentalism and the Evolution of Citizen Participation in Canada," *Alternatives: Perspectives on Society, Technology and Environment* 19, no. 1 (October 1992): 34-41. Quotation from p. 39.

29. Frank Tester, p. 39.

30. Brian Elliot notes that environmentalism has become the new scapegoat for capitalism's failures, with statements such as: "The Stalins of greenery will stop capitalism from conquering world poverty, just as socialism did." Opening remarks to a series of presentations in the Sociology of Environment, Meetings of the Canadian Sociological Association, Charlottetown, 1992.

31. "Hearings on Projects Geared to Vocal Lobbies, MLA Says," *The Edmonton Journal,* November 19, 1989.

32. T. Corcoran, *The Globe and Mail,* Report on Business, March 6, 1990.

33. Ray Kemp, "Planning, Public Hearings and the Politics of Discourse," in John Forester, ed., *Critical Theory and Public Life* (Cambridge: Massachusetts Institute of Technology Press, 1985), pp. 177-201. Quotation from p. 177.

34. Brian Wynne, *Rationality and Ritual: The Windscale Inquiry and Nuclear Decisions in Britain* (Chalfont St. Giles, England: The British Society for the History of Science, 1982), pp. 160-161.

35. Brian Wynne, p. 161.

36. Natalie Zemon Davies, "The Reasons of Misrule," in N. Z. Davies, *Society and Culture in Early Modern France* (Stanford: Stanford University Press, 1975), pp. 97-123. Quotation from p. 123.

If you walked into a hearing in progress, you would see . . .
(Photograph courtesy of *The Athabasca Advocate*)

CHAPTER 2

The Hearings

In appearing before this panel, we feel very degraded. We also feel that after a whole lifetime of work to develop a viable farming operation for our family, we now have to appear in front of this group of strangers and beg them to save our family heritage, farming operation, and our livelihood for ourselves and our family. (Tony Zachkewich, Prosperity: 7335)[1]

I feel uncomfortable that we [Alberta-Pacific] have had to lower ourselves to the public hearing process . . . . I think the criticism is a disgrace. (Stuart Lang, President of Crestbrook Forest Industries, Alpac's parent company)[2]

In this chapter, we consider the reactions of the public to the scope and structure of the Alpac public hearings. Public partici-pants raised so many questions that it is hard to believe they were fooled into displaying public support for the process simply by participating in it. In considering the questions raised, we will show how complex and dynamic the hearings were. People spoke not only to state their response to the proponent's claims about the mill's environmental impact, or their opinions about the desir-ability of the mill, but also to debate with the government, the hearing board, the proponent, and one another about whether their participation could have any effect; about who spoke for the public; about whether the hearings were conducted at a reasonable pace; and about how the government could both promote the project and conduct an environmental review of it. In a sense, the hearings were not bounded by the walls of the rooms in which they were conducted. Issues were reported and debated in news articles and broadcasts, in editorials, letters to the editor, and interviews with government officials and members of environmental organizations, and in the provincial legislature. Opinions expressed in the media and in previous sessions of the hearings were incorporated into presentations made at later sessions. Thus, there were more participants than those who spoke at the hearings, and an examination of the hearings requires that we avoid looking at each submission isolated from all the rest, but rather consider how all participants—board members, company representatives, public participants, government officials, media people, and people who discussed the hearings in letters to the editor, in schools, and in coffee shops—influenced one another's thinking and choice of words.

Structure and Scope

The chairman of the Review Board explained to public participants at the outset that the hearings would be formal, but only formal enough to get the job done:

> The Review Board does not wish to be overly formal in the procedures that we'll be using in these hearings. The hearings are non-judicial, but we believe they must be somewhat structured in order to be efficient and effective. They will be conducted in a non-confrontational manner. We'll be questioning each other, not cross-examining each other. Participants are not required to have legal counsel present, although you are welcome to do so if you wish, and the rules will be the same for everyone. (Gerry DeSorcy, Fort McMurray: 7)

If you walked into a hearing in progress, you would see the Review Board of seven men and one woman sitting at a table facing the public; sometimes, the Board was seated on a stage. The Alpac representatives, their lawyer, and their technical experts occupied one or two tables to the right of the Board. Numerous Alpac consultants—all of whom were male—sat in the audience, and were called to testify or comment on issues raised by members of the public at various times during the hearing process. Members of the Secretariat and court reporters who transcribed the proceedings occupied the tables to the left of the Board. The presenters either sat across from the Alpac representatives, on the same side as the reporters, or asked questions from a podium directly facing the

Review Board. They had to speak into microphones and their words were recorded. There was an array of microphones at each table and podium, as well as various audio-visual aids, such as overhead and slide projectors, on the stage. Often, reporters stationed themselves throughout the audience and alongside the stage, with video cameras and lights, audio recorders, and laptop computers. Power cords were everywhere.

> To the panel and to the public, and to the 14 business suits that are here in this informal, non-intimidating setting that you have set up for us and the public, thank you very much. (Kristin Reed, Fort McMurray: 527)

Despite the chairman's assurance that the rules would be the same for everyone, the structure of the hearings seemed to some people to give the proponent an unfair advantage.

> I hadn't expected for the pulp mill to have a strong representation there. That surprised me a little bit. Not only did they have a member sitting on there [the stage], they had a whole battery of people in the background. . . . I guess I envisaged more a neutral body. That's what the panel would be . . . then, to see the pulp mill representative there and fielding questions and smoothing over things and the guy coming to me afterwards in some sort of a veiled challenge, you know, "where did you get this stuff?" Almost like this is damaging information and we're going to watch you sort of thing. (Arnold Labrentz)[3]

The Alberta government's handling of the Alpac proposal was put on trial at the hearings as much as the company's claims about the environmental impact of the project. For example, one speaker asked why the public should have to show that the mill would be harmful in order to stop its construction. Why didn't the government and the company have to prove to the public that the mill would be safe?

> [W]hat is the purpose of going through this exercise [hearings]? . . . [W]hy do we have to try and convince government and Alpac that there should be further studies done before the mill or such projects go ahead? It should

be up to the government and Alpac to come to the people
of the area and prove to us beyond any reasonable doubt
that what they are proposing to do is going to be safe and
not harm us in any way, shape or form . . . they are the ones
that have the experts. The people of this area are not
experts. It's much harder for us to try and argue a case
against someone that should be out there and providing the
selling job to us. (Tony Punko, Executive Director,
Athabasca Tribal Corporation, Fort Chipewyan: 1647)

Many participants expressed reservations about the hearings,
fearing that they were window dressing for a decision already made
by government and industry, and pointing out that they hadn't been
consulted until an agreement had been reached.

Before I feel confident in any development project in
general, and Alpac in particular, the following would have to
be implemented: I would like to see an EIA process that is
legislated. I would like to see an EIA process that is
conducted by a neutral body of qualified experts, not the
company and not the government. . . . I would like to see an
EIA process that acknowledges that we are evaluating the
impact of a development on an integrated ecosystem,
rather than a bunch of individual resources that exists solely
for our buying and selling purposes. So the FMA [forest
management area] has to be part of the EIA. I would like to
see an EIA process that ensures and actively supports
meaningful public involvement at the outset of any development, rather than after the economic deals have been struck
behind closed doors. (Jody McElligott, Athabasca: 2425)

McElligott's presentation makes another criticism shared by
many other speakers: that the environmental effects of forestry
activities undertaken to supply the pulp mill were not included in
the Review Board's mandate. In light of the size of the forest
management area—73,000 square kilometres—many people thought
that the hearings were fundamentally flawed by this omission.

Forestry has said, without any serious discussion on the
matter, forestry FMAs are simply a contractual business
arrangement between us and the company, and we do not

need any third party advice as to what should or should not be in those FMAs. That has been the bottom-line message we have got from Forestry. So thank you, but no thank you. (Jerome Slavik, for Athabasca Tribal Council, Janvier: 701)

Mr. Fjordbotten [Minister of Alberta Forestry, Lands and Wildlife] has refused to even allow his scientists to attend, in spite of numerous requests from the panel. Why? . . . If Mr. Fjordbotten treats a top notch panel this way in full view of public scrutiny, we can well imagine how he will treat us and our concerns when the panel's job is complete. . . . We know with certainty who represents the interests of forestry in our government. The big question is: Who represents us? (Brief by Prosperity Environmental Association, Prosperity: 7492)

Over the last twenty years, many people in the north have become familiar with the regulations governing the oil and gas industry. They often compared the extensiveness of the public review and regulations for that industry with the Alpac review, and its lack of a forestry component. These comparisons were significant, because the chairman of the Alpac Review Board was also chairman of the Energy Resources Conservation Board, which conducted public reviews of the petroleum industry:

In the oilpatch, when we drill a critical sour gas well, we're obliged to get the acceptance of the people in that immediate area. If we can't do that, then we have to go to public hearings and address their concerns. There we are talking of a well site that could be a couple of hectares in size, critical sour gas hydropath area that might be a few hundred square kilometres in size, maybe affecting a hundred people. Yet here [Alpac FMA] we have an area that's several thousand kilometres in area and can affect several thousand people and yet we are not conducting any sort of an EIA and, therefore, it's not being addressed at the public hearings. This does not make any sense to me. (Peter Zimmerman, Athabasca: 3448)

Handcuffed by a mandate struck by the federal and provincial environment ministers, the Review Board could only listen to complaints about the virtual exclusion of forestry issues from its purview, with the exception of forestry on native lands, an area of federal responsibility. The omission was of particular concern to those who requested an ecosystem approach to the EIA process:

[W]e don't want to see it [an EIA] compartmentalized into different subject areas. We don't want it broken down into air, water and then timber harvesting, and then the mill site. (Ralph Makokis, Beaver Lake: 1280)

There does seem to be a problem . . . that our white scientific community seems to want to analyse things in isolation. They want to, so to speak, isolate the hind foot of the moose and analyse it, and then they want to analyse the sulphur, and then they want to analyse the carbon dioxide. Then they are going to analyse some other component. We have reason to believe that . . . everything is connected and interrelated and interdependent. The people on this planet are part of that interdependency. (Jim Rogers, Representative of the Trappers Association, Athabasca: 3136)

The Board agreed with such criticisms of its mandate, and said so in its report:

The principle of using an ecosystem approach to environmental management demands more holistic terms of reference. . . . An ecosystem approach is one which includes full consideration of all components of the environment and of the proposed development at once, rather than an approach which attempts to analyse different components in isolation. . . . This clearly implies the need for inclusion of forestry harvesting in the environmental review. The suggestion that such a review can be done separately—at a later time by a separate agency—seems to the Board to violate the principles of good environmental impact assessment and of good management. (Review Board Report: 77)[4]

Ironically, as the Alpac hearings proceeded, so did Alpac. While the public was considering Alpac's EIA, and the Review Board was deliberating on the information brought forward by communities, and before the Review Board issued its recommendations, Alpac was busy buying more land in the proposed site area, obtaining a local development permit, ordering equipment, preparing the mill site and clearing for services; and the utilities were laying their lines. Directing her comments to the Alpac representatives, one woman observed:

> I can see the level of confidence over there and I understand where it comes from . . . the bids are out on road construction three weeks ago for this mill. There are ads in the Athabasca local paper for workers for road building. I guess the government hasn't told them yet that this is not a sure thing. (Kristin Reed, Fort McMurray: 527)

When people made presentations at the hearings, the Review Board might be attentive, but would it make any difference to their governments? Was the political decision already made and was the public merely acting out their role in a charade? One person who thinks the hearing process is thoroughly political told us:

> There were so many fudge factors involved [in the Alpac hearings]. But I think in all of them there are sufficient fudge factors that politicians can weasel their way out of it, if they don't like it in the end. And, in a way, I guess that is a real function of the public hearings, it tells the politicians how the public is reacting. They might not be able to find out otherwise. (Jack Van Camp)[5]

Another speaker, who was familiar with Energy Resources Conservation Board (ERCB) hearings, said:

> I think the most devastating aspect of the ERCB hearing process is the inevitability of the outcome. Industry always is given the go-ahead, albeit with increasing requirements for mitigation. . . . Please do not let your decision here be a political one. We can't afford a political decision that merely requires mitigation. There is too much at stake. (Vivian Pharis, for the Alberta Wilderness Association, Edmonton: 4460-4461)

Pharis argues that mitigation, which appears politically neutral, is actually a tool used by governments to favour the dominant interests—the developers.

Who Is the Concerned Public?

> I promise to consider all of your submissions, to deal with them, to think about the ideas, the values, the analysis, the recommendations and the views that you have given us. That applies to Alberta-Pacific, it applies to the various governments, federal, provincial, territorial, municipal, and especially it applies to members of the public. Without the public, there would be no public hearings. (Bill Ross, Review Board member, Prosperity: 7626)

Despite Ross's assurance, a debate boiled, both inside the hearings and out, over which sectors of the public had more legitimate concerns, and who could speak for the public. At the hearings in Athabasca, an environmentalist who is also a retired sheep farmer and mathematics professor, Louis Schmittroth, offered a global view of the "concerned public," and a local farmer, Stan Wiskel, a narrower view:

> Wiskel: I'd like to talk about involvement, it seems to me that everybody wants to call themselves "the public." I would like to know who the public is. Is it me here, is it that gentleman sitting there, is it the Friends of the Athabasca, or is it the 1500 people that came to the mill rally [in support of the project] last summer?[6] Or is it everybody?

> Schmittroth: . . . [Y]ou mentioned, who is the public? Is it the Friends of the Athabasca? Is it the pulp mill rally? Whatever it is. Well I maintain it's all of us.

> Wiskel: I will allow that it's all of us, and it's not necessarily the people that speak the loudest.

> Schmittroth: Well, it's neither you or me right? It's not only the people of Alberta, it's the people of Canada. Not only that, it's the people of the world and everybody that is concerned about this issue. Is that not true?

> Wiskel: In diminishing order, yes. (Athabasca: 3020, 3026)

The question of whose views were to be considered legitimate was important, because opinions on the mill were divided between local and downstream communities. While the Review Board began the hearings in communities downstream from the mill site, and was made aware of many concerns of northerners far from the "epicentre" of the development, Alpac's lawyer argued that:

[T]he concerns of the people most immediately affected by a major development like this are the most important people in this sort of project, because they are the ones whose community is fundamentally changed by a project of this type and of this magnitude. (Dennis Thomas, Prosperity: 7572)

The Board, however, was reluctant to restrict the "concerned public" to members of the Athabasca community:

This is not just an Alberta issue. It's the Northwest Territories. In historical times, if somebody dumped poison into your water, then there was war. Now, this issue includes the Northwest Territories, and people downstream have a great deal of economic loss if this kind of thing is going on down here. (Cindy Gilday, Review Board member, Athabasca: 3027)

In its report, the Review Board recognized that the majority of public presentations were "entirely or partially against the project or some major part of it. . . . While a large number of residents in the Athabasca area were in favour of the project, many who appeared at the hearings were not."[7] The fact that many of those opposed to the project appeared at the hearings, while few who favoured it did so, presented a dilemma. Were the hearings designed to attract only opponents? Was the pro-development position equally represented? Should intervenor funding be given to groups representing pro-development positions, or did Alpac represent that point of view?[8] These serious points of disagreement arose again and again in the hearings, and in the media.

Mill supporters formed the organization "Friends of the Mill" to counter the media attention given to environmental groups. The Review Board and the review process came under criticism from this group:

I am here representing the Friends of the Mill because we feel very strongly that a blatant, inexcusable and indeed biased decision has taken place with regards to equal opportunity in presenting expert testimony at these hearings. (Dale Plante, Friends of the Mill, Athabasca: 3209)

The Friends of the Mill were concerned because they had been denied intervenor funding, whereas other local groups, which had expressed concerns about the project, had received such funding. The Government of Alberta, not the Review Board, was responsible for distribution of intervenor funds. When asked by the chairman to respond to Plante's comment, a government spokesman said:

We reviewed that application under a set of criteria that was used to assess all applications [for intervenor funding], and the consensus of the review [was that] the various issues that were raised in the application were either the responsibility of the proponent or the responsibility of the government. (John Shires, Alberta Environment, Athabasca: 3218)

It is interesting to note that in the struggle to win public support, the word "friends," originally used by environmental groups, such as "Friends of the Earth," because of its connotations of helping and not harming, was appropriated by the pro-mill group to help sway public opinion to its side.

Public participants debated how seriously one another's opinions should be taken, and sought to convince the Review Board to ignore or devalue the opinions of one group or another.

There are many people that are coming forward to express their personal opinions about development of this mill near Athabasca, and we think that's a good thing to a point. It provides some knowledge upon which you can measure the social impact of such a large project. But personal opinions are hardly satisfactory for measuring an environmental impact just by themselves. We must hear from the scientists, those who make a career from study of the environment; those who know how to measure environmental impact effectively. Unfortunately . . . it is the highly emotional statements that catch the attention of the media instead of the cold, hard scientific facts that may be dull and difficult to understand. (Mr. Jones, Alberta Construction Association, Edmonton: 4309-4310)

Some of the presentations that are pro the development have talked about, you know, they want to hear the hard, cold facts and not to be emotional. I would say that the cold, hard facts I have seen suggest that if you aren't emotional, perhaps you don't have any business making these decisions. (Judy Evaski-McLean, Edmonton: 5650)

Questions were raised about who is really concerned about the environment. Some presentations and letters to the editor in the Athabasca papers questioned the motives of environmentalists, and the genuineness of their concern for the environment.

If these [other environmental] concerns are not addressed by these environmentalists, then perhaps the real concerns associated with the proposed pulp mill cannot be justified as legitimate concerns, but rather as a means of personal attention. (Walter Harrynuck, Mayor, Village of Boyle, Prosperity: 7456)

[I]t must be nice to jump on a bandwagon especially if no one has been paying attention to you and you are craving for attention. By this I mean those so called friends of the Athabasca! Are they true friends of the Athabasca or are they craving for media attention such as they are getting now? (Douglas Veron)[9]

Veron went on to question the life-style of a local environmentalist "who drives a Land Rover, which, when he starts her up, would be banned in Los Angeles," and asked, "what about the farmers who are members . . . [and] insist on using diesel tractors, insecticides, herbicides, and a dozen other 'cides' that leach through the earth and into our streams, lakes and rivers?"

Several presenters took pains to explain that although most public participants were opposed to the mill, that position was not shared by a majority of local residents.

We wish the committee to take note of the fact that without exception, as far as we are aware, the mill developments are supported by all Chambers of Commerce and town and county government organizations in the region as representing a major opportunity for the region to expand its economic base, and improve the social and economic opportunities and facilities which are available to us.

In comparison, the number of those who are opposed to the proposed developments is extremely small. . . . We are concerned that actions for the public good may be unduly influenced by this tiny but vocal minority, and we urge that the opinions of the huge, but less vocal, majority take precedence. (Phil Rowlands, Athabasca Chamber of Commerce, Athabasca: 2923, 2925)

On both sides of the issue, people gave ancestry and long-term residence in the community as a reason for thinking that their opinions represented those of the majority:

I have been a rate-payer in Athabasca county for 17 years. I am retired and a grandmother of almost four grandchildren who are living here . . . I do not want this mill. It is too big and too polluted. Thank you. (Annemarie Schmittroth, Athabasca: 2383)

I have owned and operated my own business in the area for the last ten years. My father was Frank Lafferty from Lafferty Bouvier family, a well known native family throughout the north. My mother was Beatrice Rose Lepine . . . born and raised in the north. My father was a much respected riverboat pilot on the Athabasca River. . . . My parents were married at Athabasca Landing in 1913. . . . As a native person, I will always remember what Billy Mills said one time . . . we must learn to walk with one spirit in both worlds. I think it's time that our native people and other people in the community of Athabasca take advantage of oppor- tunities . . . I believe that I represent the majority of the ordinary citizens of this town [Athabasca] when I say that we are enthusiastic about the prospect of having work for our people, and we believe that the mill can be brought into this community and the environment can remain safe for us to continue to live here. (Fran Hanna, Athabasca: 2388)

Board member Chief Boucher of the Fort McKay Band, north of Athabasca, asked Hanna about native bands living downstream:

Boucher: I couldn't help but note when you made your presentation that you referred to . . . your native ancestry coming from Fort Chipewyan. We just came from up north. We had some concerns expressed about the pulp mill in those areas. I couldn't help but also note the fact that you expressed some strong support for the Alberta-Pacific mill. Would you support the pulp mill if it was shown to be a detriment to the people of the north?

Hanna: Of course I wouldn't, in that case. What I'm saying is that I have not had any concrete evidence to show that it's going to be detrimental. . . . I am concerned about the environment as a native person, probably more so than a lot of people who are being so vociferous . . . I have a vested interest in this community. (Athabasca: 2393-2394)

Hearings Without Walls

Throughout the hearings, people continued to debate the economic and environmental issues, and often referred in their presentations to what had been said at other hearing locations or in the media. Thus, the hearing cannot be seen as a simple, linear process, enclosed within the walls of the hearing rooms.

I'm personally dismayed that we still see statements coming out in the press, and now I'll quote from the Edmonton Journal November 30th, just a couple of days ago, where we have Mr. Fenner [Vice President, Pulp] saying: "If you turn this down, I think it would be a terrible message to the entire economy. It would be basically saying the most environ-mentally-sensitive mill that can ever be built is not allowed." . . . I personally and deeply resent you making these kinds of statements that are, in effect, dividing and putting Albertans against Albertans. This is the kind of scare tactic that your industry, which has a reputation among not only environmentalists but Canadians in general, as being one of the dirtiest in the country, has been making repeatedly. (Ray Rasmussen, for the Canadian Paperworkers Union, Edmonton: 5342-5343)

Just days before the hearings came to the "big city," Edmonton, Alpac tried to counter the effective criticism filtering down from the small hearing sites in the north. Alpac mounted a defence of its project with a promotional campaign to distance itself from problems in the national pulp industry. The presenter quoted below was not duped by the twelve-page brochure inserted in the local newspaper and delivered to most homes in Edmonton:

Our members in Edmonton and area received the Alberta-Pacific brochure, "Your Questions Answered" . . . . We are not impressed by that because when we have behind us the long history of concrete experiences with these very same companies, understanding the environmental damage they have caused, understanding their record in the area of occupational health and safety, we don't want to receive anything that contains bland assurances. We would rather put our faith in strong concrete language in collective agreements or, better yet, well-worded, strongly-enforced laws and regulations. (Winston Gereluk, for the Alberta Federation of Labour, Edmonton: 5298-5299)

Outside the hearing process, Alpac's executives spoke at numerous forums in an effort to quell public concern. The woman quoted here heard the company spokesmen at a public forum contradict what she had heard at the hearings. She realized the need to make Alpac accountable for its misleading information, and wrote this letter to the Review Board:

[T]his week I heard an official [from] Alpac, Mr. G. Jackson, addressing a group of the University Women's Club, state that dioxin in small amounts is "harmless." Yet, at the hearings held at the Provincial Museum in November 1989 several scientists stated that no safe levels of dioxin had yet been found, and that its effect is cumulative. . . . I would appreciate hearing if, and how, these matters have been considered. (Muriel Clarke, Filed Document O-148: 1).

Speed and Fairness for Whom?

[I] question how seriously the government, Alpac and this panel takes this public input. How in the name of all that is good and holy am I, employed in a different occupation, supposed to read the EIA, understand it—remember we are talking leading edge technology here—and make intelligent responses to it in the 14 days between 16 October and 30 October? All this, as well as make a living . . . pretend I'm married, and pay some attention to my children. (Rod Maclean, Fort McMurray: 493)

According to Adam Ashforth, "inquiries are expected to act speedily, despite a contradictory presumption of our culture that the discovery of truth has its own rhythm."[10] In Alberta and the Northwest Territories many people were frustrated with the lack of time allowed for members of the public to inform themselves, to debate, and to think about issues before they had to make their presentations. The eleventh-hour opportunity to speak underscored a recurring public complaint about the failure of government and industry to involve communities in the planning process prior to the hearings:

[O]ne of the problems that northern communities, and particularly Indian communities, have faced when large-scale projects come on stream is that notification of those projects does not allow them sufficient time to acquire the resources to acquaint their own community members with what this project is going to be and what impacts it's going to have on them. I think that these communities . . . have experienced that with respect to the tarsands projects. As a result, the tarsands projects were seminal in the evolution of a comprehensive community-based planning process as part of the socioeconomic impact assessment process for their development. That hasn't happened in pulp and paper developments. (Jim Webb, Fort Chipewyan: 1448)

People familiar with the Mackenzie Valley pipeline hearings[11] compared that model to the Alpac hearings:

Twenty-five years ago, the Canadian government was inviting oil companies to build a 48-inch pipeline from the Beaufort Sea to Zama, along the Mackenzie Valley, across the Dene homeland. Public outcry prompted the government to hold a Mackenzie Valley Pipeline Inquiry. These hearings lasted two years and provided a real democratic process to hear the voice of all the people. Young and old, men and women, proud of their heritage, spoke with eloquence and passion of their love of the land. The final report recommended a 10-year moratorium on the construction of a pipeline. . . . .Twelve years have passed, and the Dene are now more ready to participate in the economic development of the north. Now the Dene and all other northerners living downstream from the proposed pulp mills are concerned and afraid that their lands, rivers and lakes will become a sewage ground for chemical waste. . . . Projects of such magnitude directly affecting most, if not all, Native groups in Alberta as well as other northerners require hearings at least as serious and as thorough as the Mackenzie Valley Pipeline Inquiry. (Father Camille Piché, Fort Chipewyan: 1462-1463)

[I]n native communities . . . decision-making is a slow process. It's not like decision-making in non-Native communities. Once people have information, they have to think about it for some period of time, discuss it among themselves, and arrive at what they feel are the best ways to approach that. That time isn't being allowed us, we . . . would like . . . a Berger [Mackenzie Valley Pipeline Inquiry] process that would take all of the Indian communities and all of the native communities in the north into consideration in planning for these projects and allow them to plan simultaneously. (Jim Webb, Fort Chipewyan: 1449)

Some native participants criticized the way Alpac informed natives about the project, and the methods Alpac used to solicit concerns from native communities.

Alberta Pacific's methods were culturally inappropriate for obtaining our people's inputs. The values and perceptions study limited face-to-face interviews to a six-mile radius around the proposed mill site. The Public Participation Program volume (page 3.9) admits that the views of Native/Metis communities were not obtained through the open house technique, and it is concluded [by Alpac] that the views from the Native community are better obtained through meetings with Native leaders. . . . But consultation by Alberta-Pacific officials with Tribal Chiefs Association leadership amounts so far to little more than promises of employment opportunities in connection with the proposed projects and unfulfilled commitments to keep in touch as plans developed. (Ralph Makokis, Beaver Lake: 1283-1284)

As the hearings progressed, they became more costly, both to the government and to Alpac, and of course, they were "holding up development." Several people felt that the government was at fault for constantly changing the rules that the proponent had to follow, by, for example, deciding to hold a public review, deciding that the Review Board had to take into account cumulative impacts of all the pulp mills on the Peace-Athabasca river system, and deciding to expand the number of locations in which the public hearings were to be held. Alpac's lawyer protested:

Alberta-Pacific began an environmental impact assessment under a set of rules which amounted to a closed review of certain general aspects of the project by a limited number of government-employed experts. . . . Over the course of only a few months, the review . . . evolved into an intensely public examination of a much broader range of issues by several levels of government and many interest groups and affected individuals.[12]

This protest was echoed by mill supporters:

Our only regret is that our Alberta government, in its exuberance and shortsightedness, has waved the flag of opportunity and welcome without full intention of following through on its invitation. . . . We, the public, are not ignorant to the fact that the goal posts of this game have moved many, many times since December of last year. We commend you, the members from Alberta-Pacific, for your patience and your perseverance. (Dale Plante, Friends of the Mill, Prosperity: 7473-7474)

Can Government Sit in Judgement of Itself?

> Since the County of Athabasca has already shown its bias by
> granting Alpac a permit to begin construction without
> environmental approvals, how could this minister rely upon
> the County of Athabasca to make impartial recommend-
> ations for board memberships and for funding public
> intervenors?[13]

This question, addressed by an opposition environment critic to
the environment minister in the Alberta Legislature, referred to the
provincial government's initial plan to assign to Athabasca county
administration the responsibility for appointing local residents to
the Review Board, and for distributing intervenor funding. Public
outcry over conflicts of interest forced a Board member and two
alternates to resign, and the responsibility for distributing
intervenor funding was shifted to Alberta Environment.

Public distrust of the hearing process centred around the fact that
the government was undertaking actions to promote pulp mill projects to diversify the provincial economy at the same time as it was
attempting to conduct a credible environmental review of its own
development scheme. To improve the odds for a fair hearing, many
people had pushed for federal representation on the Review Board,
hoping that federal responsibility for the Northwest Territories and
for issues related to native lands, would check the self-interest of the
Province of Alberta. Given that the province staked $75 million for
infrastructure and $400 million in debentures for the project before
it began its environmental review, many people thought the
government was putting the economy ahead of the environment.

> Our provincial and municipal governments have shown that
> they are hell-bent on economic development at any cost,
> including the inestimable cost of damage to the
> environment and to quality of life, by soliciting pulp mill
> development on a vast scale. I'm talking about my family's
> environment, and my family's quality of life. And not for
> one moment do we believe that Alpac has our best interests
> at heart. They don't address the issues of what effect the mill
> will have on the quality of life and the quality to the
> environment of those that find themselves living in the
> vicinity of a huge bleached kraft pulp mill, with all the

contaminants that mill will introduce. They can't deal with
these issues because they involve a different kind of
valuation system. Money is their motivating factor. We are
relying on you, the Review Board, to fully address these
human issues, and assign them the same weight as other
considerations. People are a resource too, a resource we
cannot afford to abuse. (Merilyn Peruniak, Athabasca: 3324)

Others defended the provincial government and the ability and
authority of government experts and bureaucrats to deal with
forestry issues and protect citizens from harmful pollution:

[W]e fully expect the Provincial Department of Environment to police the development and operation of the mills
so that any adverse environmental impact will be at a
minimum. (Phil Rowlands, Athabasca Chamber of
Commerce, Athabasca: 2922)

In defending the government agencies, one man expressed his
feeling that civil servants should not have their work critically
examined by the public in the hearings:

I have complete confidence that our forests and our
environment are in safe hands, so to speak. And I trust
explicitly the willingness and the capability of these people
to guide and regulate the development of a pulp industry in
Alberta . . . I am referring to . . . our provincial development
officers, our foresters, our wildlife technicians . . . I do not
accept, and I seriously question, the validity and the wisdom
of placing these people on trial at these hearings. About the
only sin that one could accuse them of is the simple mistake
in not keeping the public informed about their efforts.
(Roman Bizon, Athabasca: 2398)

Similarly, local government representatives expressed their trust
in the provincial government's ability to protect the environment:

We also feel that our Government has the capability to
monitor and ensure that our environment is protected and
will be protected, and still be able to have economic growth
in our areas. (Bill Kostiw, Administrator, County of
Thorhild, Athabasca: 2600)

The County believes that out of the Environmental Impact Assessment and related studies done by Alpac, the input of interested parties to this board and the expertise of the Department of Environment will come a set of standards for clean air and clean water that will place Alberta in the forefront of environmental standards for this type of development . . . we request your sincere support in the approval and the development of this mill. (R. A. Wilkinson, Reeve, County of Athabasca, Athabasca: 2568)

Others were not so trusting. In support of the contrary view, some offered examples from their experience with government enforcement of the regulations for existing pulp mills:

When I learn that a pulp mill has been exceeding its effluent standards for months and it only receives a warning, as . . . with the Hinton [kraft pulp] mill, I feel I cannot trust my government's promises of protection. . . . I learned that people who test, treat, and monitor municipal waste water must be certified to have attained definite standards of training and experience. And the requirements for that fill a fairly large booklet. Alberta Environment was unable to provide me with regulations governing those who do parallel jobs in pulp mills, so I must assume that the rumour that I heard that there are no such regulations must be true. . . . I worry that my government is letting big business call the shots. (Ann Stiles, Athabasca: 3304)

Several residents of the East Kootenay region of British Columbia travelled, at their own expense, to testify at the hearings about their experiences with Alpac's parent company, Crestbrook Forest Industries. They were not optimistic about a government's ability to enforce environmental regulations:

British Columbia Waste Management took the company to court in '85, feeling they had a very strong case. They lost on a technicality that seriously demoralized Waste Management Branch staff and reduced its willingness to take . . . the company to court on effluent emission issues. (Marty Musser, for Residents of East Kootenay Region, Athabasca: 2776-2777)

As many speakers in this chapter have demonstrated, members of the public did not meekly accept the terms originally set for the hearings, but fought to wrest some control from the proponent and the government over venues, over the scope of the review, over definitions of legitimacy. The next chapter shows how they also sought to wrest control over language from the pro-development forces.

Notes

1. All items identified as "Filed Documents" are written submissions to the Alpac EIA Review Board, a collection of the Filed Documents is housed in the Athabasca University Library; quotations from the Alberta-Pacific EIA Review Board public hearings are from J. G. Moore and Associates Ltd., *The Alberta-Pacific Environment Impact Assessment Review Board Public Hearing Proceedings, Volumes 1-55* (Edmonton, Alberta: J. G. Moore and Associates Ltd., 1989).

2. "Crestbrook head frustrated with public criticism," *Kootenay Advertiser,* December 11, 1989, p. 4.

3. Follow-up interview with hearings presenter, Arnold Labrentz, Fort Smith, NWT. September 1992.

4. This and all further citations of the Review Board Report in this chapter refer to Alberta-Pacific Environmental Impact Assessment Review Board, *The Proposed Alberta-Pacific Pulp Mill: Report of the EIA Review Board, March 1990* (Edmonton, Alberta: Alberta Environment, 1990).

5. Follow-up interview with hearings presenter, Jack Van Camp, Fort Smith, NWT. September 1992.

6. The rally was organized by a local church minister and realtor, who was on retainer to Alpac. Before attending the rally, Environment Minister Ralph Klein visited with fifteen families in Prosperity to hear their concerns about the siting of the mill in their farming community.

7. Review Board Report, pp. 17-18.

8. Before the Board was established, the cabinet of the Alberta government declared that it would not give environmental groups any assistance. A decision was made later, however, to allocate intervenor funding totalling some $306,000, to public groups and native communities. Paul Edwards, *The Al-Pac Review Hearings: A Case Study* (Edmonton, Alberta: The Environmental Law Centre, 1990), pp. 83-96.

9. D. Veron, Letter to the Editor, *The Athabaskan,* December 11, 1989.

10. A. Ashforth, "Reckoning Schemes of Legitimation: On Commissions of Inquiry as Power/Knowledge Forms," *Journal of Historical Sociology 3,* no. 1 (March 1990): 1-22. Quotation from p. 10.

11. See Mr. Justice Thomas Berger, *Northern Frontier, Northern Homeland: The Report of the Mackenzie Valley Pipeline Inquiry* (Ottawa: Supply and Services Canada, 1977).

12. From the Alberta-Pacific final submission, Review Board Report, p. 11.

13. Grant Mitchell, MLA Edmonton-Meadowlark, Liberal Environment Critic questioning Environment Minister Ralph Klein *Alberta Hansard,* 22nd Legislature, First Session, no. 38 (July 14, 1989): 760.

Farmland staked for pulp-mill construction
(Photograph courtesy of *The Athabasca Advocate*)

CHAPTER 3

Sustainable Development or Unsustainable Exploitation?

Our company believes in the Brundtland Commission message, which is sustainable development, development with the highest quality environmental standards and using renewable sustainable resources . . . our standards will set, in an environmental sense, world-class emission levels. They will be ahead of the targets of other countries, countries like Sweden. Our mill . . . will be in a position to be the leading-edge technology in pulp and paper in the world. (Gerry Fenner, Vice President Pulp, Alberta-Pacific, Edmonton: 4287-4288)[1]

Carefully define your working terms. You will use the phrase "sustainable development" and "integrated resource management" and so will the company. The only problem will be that your vision and theirs will not be the same. The words will be the same; the meanings will be somehow very different. (Leslie Giroday, Residents of East Kootenay Region, Athabasca: 2760)

Our Common Future, the Report of the World Commission on Environment and Development published in 1987, recognized the earth as a planet in distress. The authors of the report realized that the natural systems of earth have a finite capacity to supply the production and consumption demands of capitalism and global population growth. But they also believed that continued industrial development is necessary to relieve poverty and supply the basic needs of all people. The report, often called the "Brundtland Report," after the Commission's chairman, Gro Brundtland, championed sustainable development as a way of meeting the need for both economic development and environmental protection.[2]

The phrase "sustainable development" has an immediate appeal. It sounds like a noble goal, one worth striving for, and it suggests that we can have everything we want all at once, including a healthy environment and economic well-being. In the 1990s, there is great pressure on everyone—politicians, policy makers, business people and environmentalists alike—to support both sustainability and development. It is hard to imagine anyone gaining a large measure of public support for a position that openly favours one to the detriment of the other. But the phrase means different things to different groups, depending on whether they stress environmental sustainability or economic development. As William Rees explains:

> [T]o some, sustainable development is a long awaited call for political recognition of environmental decay, economic injustice, and limits to material growth . . . an opportunity for humanity to correct an historical error and begin a more benign, balanced, stable relationship with the natural world . . . [sustainable development] also raises moral considerations such as the need in a finite world for an equitable sharing and conservation of its natural bounty.[3]

On the other hand, Rees identifies a contradictory and equally powerful message in the Brundtland Report, a message that equates sustainable development with "more rapid economic growth in both industrialized and developing countries" on the grounds that:

> [E]conomic growth and diversification . . . will help developing countries mitigate the strains on the rural environment, raise productivity and consumption standards, and allow nations to move beyond dependence on one or two primary products for their export earnings.[4]

When the Government of Alberta announced the $1.3 billion Alpac pulp-mill project, it claimed to be diversifying the economy by exploiting an underutilized renewable resource—the boreal forest of northern Alberta. Quoting from the Brundtland Report, Alberta's Minister of Forestry, Lands and Wildlife, LeRoy Fjordbotten, spoke of sustainable development as creating a harmonious relationship among investment, technological development, and development of Alberta's renewable resource industry, to meet the needs of both the present and the future.[5] As the opening quote for this chapter demonstrates, Gerry Fenner, Alpac's Vice President Pulp, used superlatives, such as "leading-edge technology," "world-class emission levels," and "highest quality environmental standards," to lend credence to his claim that the project represented sustainable development. He used these terms to make Albertans feel proud about their partnership in this pulp mill. Rather than present the pulp mill in the larger context of world pulp prices, Alberta's low stumpage fees, an accommodating provincial government, and the mill's capacity for huge volumes of trees, Fenner directed his audience's attention to the glamour of the mill's technology. He also excited Albertans by alluding to a global competitive advantage in environmental standards, and compared Alberta to Sweden, a country that evokes the image of a clean environment, an advanced, caring government, and a prosperous economy.

Environmentalists argue that the use of the expression "sustainable development" can mask and make more palatable what Rees describes as the second message of the Brundtland Report—more rapid economic growth. Just as the promotion of environmentally friendly consumer products shifts emphasis from consumption to a contribution to a better environment, so the use of the phrase "sustainable development" implies that economic development is justified environmentally. This legitimation of development tends to placate the public, and to reinstate industry and government into positions of authority and trust.

However, in Alberta, a significant proportion of the public was not satisfied with the notion of sustainable development presented by government and industry as underpinning pulp, paper, and forestry expansion in the northeast region of the province. In June 1989, 12,000 Albertans signed a petition asking for a moratorium on pulp mills because of environmental concerns. J. Stanley Rowe, who spoke in March 1989 at the Workshop on Bleached Kraft Pulp Mill Technology and Environmental Issues, brought a global perspective to thinking about sustainable development. Rowe focused, not on the glamour of new technology, but on "worsening global problems that stem from local and incremental actions":

[I]n every region . . . people armed with powerful technology are knocking ecosystems apart and using the pieces to feed huge ever-growing industries which then excrete garbage, sometimes in our faces, sometimes in more subtle ways. . . . The eating up and the spewing out are all incremental, taking place every day here and there and everywhere, mostly by little bites and little bits, making it difficult to trace the sources and assess the magnitude of the danger. Deforestation to feed mills is part of a world-wide problem.[6]

As we saw in Chapter 1, the purpose of environmental public hearings in Canada is to help make decisions that will favour both economic development and environmental protection. It is not surprising, then, that the debate over the Alpac project often centred on whether or not the project represented "sustainable development." This chapter examines the public's response to four economic figures of speech used by government and industry in this debate: "window of opportunity," "a forest of weeds," "market forces," and "hard economic facts." We also discuss the responses of some native groups to Alpac's assessment of the mill's economic impact on native people.

A Window of Opportunity?

It has . . . been almost a year since we started the public involvement process and began our EIA work. We have, because of our project timing, entered into the process in the beginning of what I would call a transition period. This has resulted in uncertainty in timing, scoping and costs . . . the window of opportunity for us closes rapidly. (Gerry Fenner, Prosperity: 7620)

Sustainable development . . . taken to heart means working back from the needs of the forest to the supplies for mills and not, as is normal, from the demands of mega-mills to the forest as forced-growth supplier. (J. Stanley Rowe)[7]

Under pressure to respond to shifts in the global economy, the Alberta government and other western Canadian provincial governments have been seeking new trading and investment partners, especially in Southeast Asia. Faced with the ups and downs of the oil industry and a less than healthy agricultural sector, Alberta's Conservative government seized on forestry developments to promote a new industrial base for the province. According to an Edmonton Economic Development Authority representative:

> [T]here is . . . a need for the creation or expansion of propulsive industries, such as the pulp and paper industry, which will stimulate entrepreneurial activity. These propulsive industries are characterized by large-scale plants and export orientation, capital-intensive production, high technology and a highly-trained work force. . . . Alberta Pacific. . . has the linkages within the economy that will enable a broadening of the northern Alberta industrial base, provide the opportunity for existing firms to broaden their range of products, services and technology, and also set the scene for further new endeavours such as environmental control businesses and technologies. . . . [C]omparative price movements show that pulp and paper markets appear to be independent of oil and gas markets, often counter-cyclical to oil and gas markets, and possibly more predictable than oil and gas markets. It is the counter-cyclical and predictable nature of these markets in particular that will enable additions to Alberta's pulp and paper industry to have an enhanced stabilizing effect on the economy. (Rick Hursak, Edmonton Economic Development Authority, Edmonton: 4368-4370)

In order to attract foreign investors, the Alberta government offered financial assistance. Alpac pocketed $250,000 to finance its feasibility study, $75 million for road and rail infrastructure, and $400 million in government debentures.[8] Such assistance led Adam Zimmerman, President of Noranda—a company which withdrew a proposed pulp mill in Tasmania because the environmental controls were too strict—to praise the Alberta government: "they kiss [pulp companies] on both cheeks and give them grants."[9]

The provincial government's own publications made the same point:

> Alberta is open for business. The Government of Alberta offers services and assistance programs and supports a free enterprise environment committed to encouraging foreign investment. Take advantage of Alberta's forest development opportunities.[10]

Business and government called the Alpac proposal a window of economic opportunity—a Canadian window on the global economy that would close forever if the Alpac proposal was denied for environmental reasons.

> Many people are asking: why is all this development occurring now? Most of it is driven by demand for hardwood pulp. . . . Companies are turning to our abundant supplies of aspen to meet their immediate needs. We have been able to capitalize on an exceptionally strong pulp market before alternative fibre suppliers are developed elsewhere.[11]

The metaphor "window of opportunity" exerted pressure inside and outside the hearing process: it was used to force public deliberation about a sustainable future into a business decision-making time frame, and to deflect the question of whether the opportunity was really golden. If the opportunity was not seized, so the argument went, dire results could follow for Albertans. Some public hearing participants objected to this last step of the argument:

> [Mr. Fenner] says, and I quote, "It could be dangerous for the Canadian economy if we turn down this project. If we turn it down, it would send a terrible message to the economic community," which, of course, is the heavy stick of blackmail which this company is trying to use in its sort of mad attempt to overcome people's choices in this matter . . . he even mentions . . . "The pulp and paper industry across Canada is nervously watching the public hearing process. . . ." Well, you bet they are because they have been ripping off Canada and other parts of the world for many years. (Ross Campbell, Edmonton: 4595-4596)

A Forest of Weeds?

[I]t's aspen; it's a weed. What are you going to use it for?[12]

We've had an aspen resource in northern Alberta that's been considered a weed and been thrown away, and all of a sudden there's a use for it.[13]

Landowners with poplar on their land will now have an opportunity to utilize this species. In the past it has been considered a weed and was generally thought of as an obstruction to be removed prior to farming. Now the landowners will have an opportunity to manage these lands for long-term profit.[14]

These quotes, the first two by LeRoy Fjordbotten, Minister of Forestry, Lands and Wildlife, and the last from an information package produced by Fjordbotten's department, indicate a view of aspen that has a long history in Alberta. In the past, when farmers cleared the boreal forest, they cursed the aspen and poplar because it suckered from the roots and re-established itself to compete with agricultural use of the land. Thus, the metaphor—aspen is a weed— implies that aspen of the boreal forest is a nuisance; has no economic value; competes with agriculture; and is vigorous and grows back even when it is ignored. The boreal forest was seen for what it was not: it was not the lucrative softwood resource of British Columbia, Ontario, and the eastern slopes of Alberta's Rockies. This view devalued the place of the boreal forest in global ecosystems, and its role as a homeland for aboriginal peoples, a habitat for wildlife, and a source of biodiversity.

Until recently, the mixed aspen and coniferous forests of Alberta's north were not considered profitable to harvest for pulp production. Hardwoods, such as aspen, were difficult to transform into high-quality pulp, and economies of scale, supply, and harvesting costs were more favourable for the softwoods of British Columbia and Eastern Canada. The declining availability of softwoods and recent changes in pulping technology have meant that suddenly Alberta's boreal forests have become economically attractive to the pulp industry. According to the Alberta Forest Service, industrial use of our mature, decaying forest will actually invigorate it, cut down the cost of fighting forest fires, and exploit a source of unrealized wealth.

An operator of a small sawmill north of Athabasca argued that the forest would go to waste if it was not used, and his sentiment was echoed by government, industry, and mill boosters:

This poplar forest has been around as long as I have been around, and a lot longer probably. It is rotting; it is dying; it

is giving off gases; it is tipping over; it is causing a breeding
ground for insects of all types. It is old; it is overmatured. . . .
You can't do nothing with it because it is too old and it is
too rotten. . . . The only thing that can use it is the pulp mill.
. . . It would create a lot of employment for a lot of children.
(Frank Crawford, Grassland: 6852)

The power of the metaphor—aspen is a weed—began to work in
new ways when the Alpac pulp mill was announced. Suddenly, the
government and the pulp and paper companies claimed to have
made something out of nothing. The boreal forest and the spindly
aspen became marketable commodities. The press dubbed aspen
the Cinderella tree, whose overlooked economic value, obscured by
the grandeur of her sister softwoods, was released by the magic
spells of technology and the marketplace. Like Cinderella's beauty,
the economic value of aspen was discovered and saved from
uselessness by Prince Charming—Alpac.

Here all the great discourses intersect: the ability of humans to
create economic growth from nothing, through technology and the
magic of the market; the abundance of nature and its infinite ability
to sustain and regenerate itself—like the weeds in our front lawns;
and the coupling of economic growth through pulp-mill development with sustainable development. These powerful images
overshadowed other views of the forest.

For example, the argument that aspen is a weed ignores the value
of the forest as a complex ecosystem. Consider how these speakers
tried to counter the dominant view, and to make the public think
critically about the spreadsheet of the market:

Forests are not just trees or cellulose factories. They are
home to thousands of kinds of living things with their own
lives to live and their own evolutionary destinies. The way
we view the land, whether or not we see ourselves as part of
the land and partner within a living community, determines
in large measure what the land can and will give us. Once
our air and water are fouled and the old growth forests are
gone, the potential for sustainable and environmentally-
sound development will have been taken away. And with
that potential, gone will be the wood warblers, the woodland
caribou, rare orchids, epiphytic lichens, marten, and countless other creatures. To maintain that trees that grow old

and die of natural causes are "wasted" is a mercenary view at best. One might also argue that old people who die of natural causes are wasted. This is nonsense. Old trees and old people enrich the lives of all living things dependent on them, be they chickadees, caribou or children. You and I and every living thing here is composed of recycled carbon that was once part of living, breathing plants and animals. The water in our bodies was once rain, snow and river water. We are the ash of a supernova and a universe filled with everyday miracles. Let us hope we can work towards greater dignity and humility and viewpoints that befit our critical role in the history of our planet. (Elizabeth Beaubien, Athabasca: 3480-3481)

This forest is not useless just because it is not being con-sumed. It serves many purposes. Climate regulation, wildlife refuge, water reservoir, air filter, nursery for many unique plants, and probably several other uses that we haven't been smart enough to figure out yet. We must learn lessons from the harm already done to the environment by man's greed. We must think of future generations. We must think of the other species that inhabit this area. What will a further polluted river [do] to the whooping cranes nesting in the Athabasca Delta? And we must realize as the animals go, so do we. (Ann Stiles, Athabasca: 3299)

The Market Made Me Do It

By our own nature, we demand a white paper that will create a better appearance for our correspondence and other requirements. Because of this demand, we . . . require a manufacturer of this nature. (Walter Harrynuck, Mayor of Boyle, Prosperity: 7454)

The usual counter to demands for more public scrutiny of private sector operations has been that the economy is democratic through the workings of the market and the exercise of "consumer sovereignty." Consumers, it is argued, can exercise effective control over the private sector by choosing products they favour and rejecting those they find inappropriate.[15]

Alpac maintained throughout the hearings that it made pulp for fine paper in response to market forces. Its clients wanted bright white paper with strong fibres; therefore, Alpac was forced to bleach pulp with chlorine. (It is the chlorine in the kraft process that produces organochlorines, including toxic dioxins and furans.) Likewise, market requirements for strong white fibres explained why, although Alpac was supportive of recycling in principle, it could not mix recycled fibres into its pulp: to do so would reduce the whiteness of pulp made from Alberta's virgin hardwood fibre.

In their study of controversies over the recent expansion of pulp mills in Western Canada, Joel Novek and Karen Kampen confirm that there is an increased global demand for laser printer, photocopy, and fax papers, and note a 105 per cent increase in the consumption of fine paper by Canadians between 1970 and 1988. "Hence the linkage between the expansion of the information industry worldwide and the announcement of pulp and paper megaprojects in the boreal forest."[16] Novek and Kampen argue that the technological fix promised by the new information society and its paperless offices turns out to have been a technocentric ideal—a sleight-of-hand that shifted our attention away from the material reality of the computer age and the real ecological costs of increased paper consumption in the 1990s: water pollution by bleaching agents used to make paper whiter; increased exploitation of forests; and the destruction of ecosystems. The market for fine paper has surpassed that for newspaper, and per capita consumption now stands at 61 kilograms per year. These facts show that there is real demand for bleached kraft paper. This was the market niche Alpac sought.

In *The Myth of the Market,* Jeremy Seabrook says that "the market" is a homely notion that adds life to the abstraction "the economy" by appealing to our everyday experiences of shopping locally or selling goods.[17] This feature of the term "market forces" made it easier for Alpac to lay blame for using bleached kraft paper on individual members of the public, especially housewives. Alpac's President, Stuart Lang, in an address to the Athabasca Chamber of Commerce, explained that it was actually women in the marketplace who drove the demand for bright white paper. The massive use of paper by business and government bureaucracies did not feature in his account. This local woman's protest accepts the framing of Lang's argument, but struggles against its conclusion:

> Open Letter to Stuart Lang Re: Your talk to the Athabasca District Chamber of Commerce January 25, 1989.
>
> Yes, you are right. Women have been responsible for the consumer demand for paper, and particularly white paper. Women do spend the majority of the family budget, and they do influence the spending of the rest of the family dollars. Thank-you for reminding us. Because in addition to our "women's work," we are now going to add paper conservation, recycling, and the use of unbleached paper to our long list of responsibilities. . . . Future generations are going to hear the aspen echo in the whispering hills of Athabasca because it is "women's work" to ensure it. And this "women's work" will get done as usual.
>
> Yours truly, Patricia F. Reiter[18]

During the hearings in Athabasca, however, another woman questioned the premise that market demand alone, and not Alpac, created unexpected pressures on natural resources, pressures that come with real costs for the environment.

> Merilyn Peruniak (Athabasca area resident): What do you base your market research on?
>
> Gerry Fenner (Vice President Pulp, Alpac): . . . the market itself.
>
> Peruniak: . . . I put it to you that within the next decade, you are going to see major changes in the bleached kraft pulp market. And I think my estimations are probably as good as yours. . . .
>
> David Schindler (Review Board member): Mr. Fenner to what extent does the pulp and paper industry determine these markets or try to drive them?

> It is my experience from soap and detergent companies and the power industry that these markets can be driven rather than predicted. They push the markets in the directions they want them to go. I once overheard one, admittedly drunken, detergent executive brag to one of his colleagues that they could package horseshit in a yellow and orange box and housewives would still buy it.
>
> Peruniak: Not this housewife! (Athabasca: 3335, 3339)

Fenner does not say what he means by "the market," but the word empowers his discourse. He presents Alpac's case as if the company made no choice or had no real options when it made a choice: no choice in targeting its market niche; no choice of bleaching process (i.e., chlorine bleaching over other processes less damaging to the environment); no choice but to reject recycling. The discourse of the market is persuasive because it makes Alpac appear subordinated to market laws and market rules that are carved in stone.

The impersonal, objective appearance of market forces combines with the already abstract corporate persona of Alpac to remove further from public awareness the agency implicit in company decision making. Because it does not create the market, we are to assume that Alpac simply responds helplessly to it. Regretting the corporation's inability to move away from chlorine bleaching, Fenner explained, "our problem has always been . . . consumer driven."[19] Following this logic to the end, it is we who actually force Alpac to pollute, because the market is you and I, the consumers of shiny white paper. We are the cause of pollution.

In the theatre of the hearing process, Schindler, a member of the Review Board, speaks out of character and breaks through this dominant discourse. His use of humour and anecdote pierces through the authority of Fenner's representation of Alpac as a victim of market forces. He reaffirms that corporate decision makers are not victims of an impersonal marketplace. His intervention reveals the existence of agents within Alpac who make market choices—choices about what they produce and how. The choice to use chlorine bleaching to make white paper is now recognizable as a grab for a highly profitable end of the paper market. The choice not to incorporate recycled paper also means that Alpac has made a choice to pollute in order to make money. Schindler has announced to Alpac that he will not accept economic rationales as a justification for evading responsibility for environmental damage.

But Schindler's anecdote not only deprives Alpac decision makers of the mask of the myth of the market. Schindler advances the counter-narrative voiced by ordinary Canadians critical of Alpac's proposal: that corporations could, if they chose to focus their efforts in this direction, create a market for unbleached or less white paper with recycled fibre content (and thus eliminate chlorine and its significant environmental damage). By unmasking the myth of an impersonal market, Schindler reasserts that corporate sales-men create markets, that they can and do manipulate consumers.

Finally, Peruniak's retort, "Not this housewife," directed at both Fenner and Schindler, asserts the sovereignty of the thinking consumer. She announces the presence in the 1990s of environ-mentally conscious people who refuse to be victims of the market or of corporate decision makers. Most importantly, she represents a kind of public criticism that extends beyond using consumer power to boycott a product such as bleached paper—her criticism extends to the company's choice of production process itself. This comment is evidence for Frank Tester's belief that a key shift has occurred: "Consumer sovereignty appears as an argument for, not against, greater public scrutiny of private-sector activities."[20]

Respect for Mother Earth

> The pulp mill will produce bleached kraft market pulp from the presently under-utilized hardwood and softwood forest resources of northeastern Alberta.(Alpac EIA Main Report: 2.1)[21]

> This you must know: this land, these forests and water, are not just resources to be harvested and managed. They were given to us to take care of and treat with respect, the way our grandfathers have always done. We are responsible for taking care of Mother Earth because Mother Earth takes care of us. Every day, we give thanks for this beautiful Mother Earth and the animals and plants that live upon her land and in her waters and skies. But we see many things wrong with Mother Earth today. We see how the oil wells are harming the water, the land and the people. The next generation must learn about the things that are wrong with

Mother Earth. They must take many important decisions about the future of our people and the land we have been given. But how can they make those decisions when they don't know their culture, when they don't have the bush to teach them about their responsibilities to our mother, the Earth? These pulp mills will take those things away from them. The land won't come back as quickly as these experts say. We have lived with this land for many generations. We know its cycles. We know it won't be the same after they take away the trees. This destruction weighs heavily on us, like a war. There is no war but we are being destroyed. You don't need a war to destroy a Native person, just take away the bush, just take away the trees. That will destroy us. The money will be all that is left. (Bigstone Cree Band Elder's Senate Statement, Filed Document O-145: 1)

During "National Forest Week" in High Level . . . Canfor district forester Brian Carnell spoke of the forest as a multi-million dollar industry. The High Level mayor spelled out the "special relationship" High Level people have with the forest: "a source of economic security, a source of jobs." Nobody mentioned the more special relationship the Aboriginal people, the Dene Tha, the Cree and the Metis have with the land, the forest, the rivers, and the wildlife. (Father Camille Piché, Filed Document E-3: 5)

There are native people living on the rivers that the Alpac mill would pollute, and drawing subsistence from the forest that would be harvested for the mill. Native people and communities were divided on the Alpac proposal. Some native people believed Alpac; some living in the area covered by the Forest Management Agreement thought they would get jobs; and some native leaders in the cities sided with the government. Others felt that Alpac would threaten their traditional way of life and undermine their relationship with nature. Alpac did not ignore the traditional native world view. Rather, it courted pro-development bands and councils, while showing respect for the bands and elders who were in opposition. The issue of traditional life-styles and the place of native values in modern society became a highly political debate.

The leadership of both the Metis Association and the Indian Association of Alberta supported the Alpac proposal. Furthermore, the Athabasca-Lac La Biche Member of the Legislative Assembly, Mike Cardinal, aggressively promoted the mill: "I as a Native MLA campaigned on this specific project, campaigned on economic diversification, and I won the election hands down."[22] On the other hand, the northern bands living in the forests to be harvested rejected the mill. For example, approximately one-third of the forest management area covers the traditional lands of the Bigstone Band and the communities they represent: Sandy Lake; North and South Wabasca Lakes; Peerless Lake; Chipewyan Lake; and Calling Lake. Most are isolated communities, not reserves. At the hearings in Wabasca, Bigstone Band Chief Charles Beaver greeted the panel with these words "We, as Bigstone Band, represent ourselves. And let it be known that the Indian Association of Alberta does not speak on our behalf."[23]

The Bigstone Chief noted that Treaty members in these communities endure unemployment rates of 80 to 90 percent, and that few received any employment from the oil and gas exploration of the last decades. In fact, "It has created a lot of negative impacts, socially, culturally, and environmentally."[24]

However, the President of the Metis Association of Alberta countered that:

> Clean air and pure water mean little to people living in futility with few opportunities and unfulfilled dreams and fading hopes. . . . Is it any wonder that we seek ways to provide opportunities for our people to become self-sufficient? Is it any wonder that we weigh the plight of our people so heavily against the potential for environmental damage? Do these who so rigorously oppose Alpac have as much at stake as we do? (Larry Desmeules, Edmonton: 4316-4317)

The Chief of the Bigstone Band was equally concerned, but he questioned whether pulp-mill developments would build self-esteem and self-sufficiency for his people. He recounted feelings of helplessness in the face of government and industry:

> [I]t seems to us that we are totally accountable to the governments, federally and provincially; yet the government is never accountable to us. Our land and its resources are held in ransom in exchange for social welfare and medical services. We must always adjust to western society's

standards. What about western society accepting our livelihood, our Native standards of how we live. . . . This [mill] is unacceptable to traditional Native standards. We cannot compromise our culture, our tradition, our history any longer. Time and time again Native people and their lands and life-style have been bulldozed over by industrial developers who see only the resources, such as natural gas, oil, coal, trees, water. . . . They neither see nor care about the people whose lives are dependent upon a clean land with abundant wildlife. (Charles Beaver, Wabasca: 6042-6043)

Mill proponents, including Mike Cardinal and other pro-development natives, often downplayed traditional uses of the forest, suggesting that the traditional life was a thing of the past:

I want to clarify a couple of issues in relation to fishing, trapping. How many trappers in the FMA area make a living trapping? My dad was a trapper. He is 75 years old now. He spent 65 years in the bush. He has trapped. He knows facts about trapping. He is one of the best trappers around. He tells me you cannot make a living trapping now. Times have changed. You have to live off the land and off the resource of the land in a different fashion; that is a modern way of harvesting the resource.[25]

Likewise, the company saw the mill's effects on trapping almost entirely in economic terms:

Trapping represents an important source of income (cash and income-in-kind) for some native people. Project operations of woodlands and pulp mill activities could disrupt trapping harvest activities at some locations, causing loss of income. To the extent that some of these disruptions are unavoidable, measures for compensation and mitigation need to be established. (Alpac EIA Main Report, Appendix 6: 6.3)

Some participants countered this economic view, and defended trapping as part of native life and local economy, not merely as a means to make money on the market by trading furs:

[T]here have been comments to this panel that the income derived from trapping and wildlife is diminishing and as a result ostensibly becoming less important in terms of income or a source of livelihood for aboriginal or Indian people. And while it is true that maybe income from trapping per se or fishing per se is down, that as an industry it probably occupies the same troubled state as your agricultural industry for white farmers. . . . But what that kind of analysis ignores is the importance of that source of food for aboriginal people. . . . In Indian country we don't have that kind of food bank, but we do have access to our fish, to our wildlife. . . . So to look at just fish and wildlife from the point of view of trapping income is to ignore . . . a very important reality of life in Indian country because that food is essential to every day survival. (Harold Cardinal, Wabasca: 6185-6187)

Non-market values of the environment are often unrecognized in debates over the economics of development. For example, spiritual and ecological understandings of the forest and nature are not valued in the cost-benefit analyses of the authors of Alpac's EIA documents. These values were mentioned, but only after economic factors, and they were never discussed in detail. Not everyone agreed that the pulp mill could co-exist with native culture:

I feel a frustration while people are talking here trying to relate the spiritual aspect of one's beliefs to the market- place that could care less what you believe and what you don't believe. (Bernie Carlson, Wabasca: 6237)

I have been in front of several panels, and I will try to make sense to the free enterprise world, the capitalists, that have a difficult time in understanding the Indian philosophy . . . our people always have the understanding that we will always be in the womb of our Mother Earth. And it's because of that understanding that we understand the chain of life that surrounds us . . . that all life is connected. And it is with that understanding that we understand what genocide means . . . what self-destruction means. (Simon Lucas, Wabasca: 6028-6029)

Some native people wondered if traditional values were respected merely because it was politically expedient to do so. To counter

Alpac's lip service to native values, the Bigstone Band strategy, as developed by the Mother Earth Healing Society, was to catalogue the broken promises of pulp companies in the past. They brought Chief Simon Lucas, a representative of the BC Aboriginal Council and BC Aboriginal Fisheries Commission, to testify:

> [I]n our area of British Columbia . . . there is a pulp mill where they have been spewing out chemicals. . . . Now they [the Mowahchat Tribe] are not allowed to harvest nothing. Everything [the fisheries] is literally closed. But they were saying to us 25 years ago that nothing would ever be tampered with. . . . They told our people that the game, the deer and the elk, would never be affected. Well, it was affected. . . . They no longer have the freedom to fish in the rivers; no longer have the freedom to roam the mountains . . . these people [the Bigstone] are placed in the same position. The moose has been planned out of the plan; the beaver has been planned out of the plan; the caribou has been planned out of the plan . . . when you start neglecting the moose and the caribou and the beaver, then you are in fact involved in genocide. (Simon Lucas, Wabasca: 6029-6031)

To alleviate concerns about adverse effects of the development, pulp-mill representatives often mentioned that they would be living in the area:

> On behalf of Alberta-Pacific, I would like to thank the elders, the Chief and councillors. We appreciate your wisdom, and we appreciate your point of view. We would like you to know that we would not build this pulp mill if we thought it would destroy our common future. By "common," I mean that we will be living here as well as you. (Gerry Fenner, Beaver Lake: 1325)

Fenner uses the phrase "our common future" to link his own health and his own future to those of the people in the communities where the mill will operate. On a number of occasions in the hearings, Fenner made testimonials about living "downstream of many pulp mills during my some 30 years in pulp mills,"[26] and enjoying good health, good hunting, and good fishing in British Columbia.

Chief Lucas dismissed the claim that the Alpac directors might share a common future with native people:

> You could in fact destroy thousands of years of life in a matter of . . . five years? Ten years? Fifteen years? And where are you going to be? Who do you think is going to be still here? When people have walked out with their millions of dollars, who do you think is going to be still here fifty years from now? It will be our people. Those foreign investors, do you think they are going to be here when all the trees are gone? Do you think, honestly . . . they will be here living amongst our people? (Simon Lucas, Wabasca: 6035)

Hard Economic Facts?

> I am convinced that the Alberta government is selling out our natural resources for a mess of pollution. In a world of ever-decreasing natural environment, our forests become an ever-more valuable asset as forests—not as providers of pulp. . . . [P]ulp mills make no economic sense, unless all the spin-off industries (e.g., paper production) are also situated in the same area. Shipping our raw pulp out of our country to be processed elsewhere is adding economic insult to environmental injury. . . . [I]t makes economic sense to hang on to a commodity that is scarce—forests, clean water, clean air. (Johanna Leenders, Filed Document N-126)

It was difficult to pin Alpac and the Alberta government down to providing a serious cost-benefit analysis of the pulp-mill project, even in traditional economic terms of investment, infrastructure costs, tax revenue, and so on. The Review Board did not insist that this analysis should be provided, and its report mirrored the majority opinion that, on balance, the mill would provide economic benefits, although it noted the reservations of some participants.[27] However, it did not mention two serious criticisms raised by public participants: exporting jobs while accepting pollution; and problems with measuring economic growth using standard indicators.

When the federal government expressed environmental concerns about the Alpac proposal, provincial politicians protested, equating the environmental concerns of Environment Canada and Fisheries and Oceans with the efforts of the Trudeau Liberals to control oil and gas development and pricing. Politicians tapped into a powerful discourse of distaste for federal intervention in areas of provincial jurisdiction—in this case, forestry. Almost lost in the acrimony was the fact that the Government of Alberta was proposing to share control of provincial forests with Japanese-owned, transnational corporations.

Despite claims that Alpac would enhance northern diversification and increase control over our natural resources and provincial economy, some people felt that we had just exchanged masters. Business analysts noted few forward economic linkages, such as quality or specialty papermaking, or sheeter mills; these jobs were in Japan and the United States. Rather, mega-mills simply reinforced the long-standing role of Canadians as "hewers of wood."[28] David Coles, national representative for the Canadian Paperworkers Union, suggested that "what we have here is a proposal to liquify Canadian trees, so we can export them as pulp to be made into paper."[29]

A member of the Pro-Canada Network linked the export of jobs to a new global division of labour in pollution:

> While employment is exported and lost to Albertans, environmental impact will be greatest at the locations where the forest reserve is harvested and transformed into pulp, that is in Alberta. To a great extent, infrastructural costs and the costs of environmental protection will be left to the Alberta taxpayer living in the exploited province, our own Alberta. (William Stollery, Edmonton: 4399)

The very name "Alberta-Pacific" helps obscure the unequal economic and environmental exchanges identified by Stollery and Coles, because it promotes the image of land-locked Alberta linked to the emerging trade block of the Pacific Rim countries, and also links Alberta with a powerful legitimating discourse: the call for economic restructuring and for globalization of the Canadian economy. The role of Alberta-Pacific, then, was to bring about this economic union and globalization.

The hyphenated title, Alberta-Pacific, suggests equal partnership in a global firm and a flow of benefits to Albertans. The aura of local ownership minimizes a strong nationalist sentiment against foreign ownership. Many people who spoke at the hearings pointed out that Alberta-Pacific is a wholly owned subsidiary of Crestbrook Forest Industries of British Columbia, which is controlled by two foreign shareholders: Mitsubishi Corporation and Honshu Paper Company, both of Japan. Each owns 32 per cent of Crestbrook.[30]

> Honshu/Mitsubishi . . . that's Alberta-Pacific in Toryspeak. (John McInnis, Official Opposition Environment Critic)[31]

> [Environmentalists] call it the Mitsubishi/Honshu project because they think we're trying to hide that the Japanese are involved. (LeRoy Fjordbotten, Minister of Forestry, Lands and Wildlife)[32]

Not just ownership, but also environmental track records were hidden behind the name. Lost within the bland non-specificity of the corporate name Alberta-Pacific were the rapacious logging practices used in Southeast Asia by the Japanese firms Mitsubishi and Honshu Paper, which were among the Japanese corporations cited by the World Wildlife Fund in 1989 as "eco-outlaws."[33] Alpac sought to distance itself from the Japanese corporations by noting that the parent firm—Crestbrook Forest Industries—was Canadian, traded on the Toronto stock exchange, and had operated a pulp mill in Skookumchuk, British Columbia, since the 1960s. On the other hand, when confronted with Crestbrook's pollution and logging infractions in British Columbia, and its poor record of native employment, Alpac sought to deflect criticism by dismissing Crestbrook's past practices as irrelevant to the current project. According to Alpac's Gerry Fenner, former manager of the Crestbrook pulp mill, "It is the policy of Alberta-Pacific not to comment on or to judge other companies."[34] The naming of Alberta-Pacific produced the effect of cleansing a corporate image:

> Crestbrook, of course, they didn't want to use their name here because they have a new name. They have laundered their name very much as Mafia might do. They have a new name now. And they are clean, they say. (Ross Campbell, Edmonton: 4600)

When pro-mill politicians and Alpac representatives spoke of the boreal forest mainly as a commodity that could be harvested to create economic wealth, they combined a particular view of the forest with influential discourses from economics about growth, investment, and job creation. Alpac provided this overview of its economic and community effects:

> The capital investment of some $1.3 billion to construct the pulp mill and related infrastructure over a three year period will bring substantial socio-economic benefits to the region. Over 20 years of operation, it is estimated that an additional $3.2 billion will be spent. Capital investment of a further $300 million to build a paper mill could also take place in response to favourable market conditions and industrial synergy. (Alpac EIA Main Report, 5.3)

Herman Daly and John Cobb, among others, argue that standard notions of economic growth, such as increasing gross national production, fail to recognize, and factor in, the adverse social and ecological costs of economic development.[35] Similarly, according to William Rees, mainstream economic models are founded upon "shared illusions" that fail to recognize that consumption of ecological resources "has begun to exceed sustainable rates of biological production."[36] David Suzuki, who spoke at the hearings at the request of the Bigstone Band, explained that:

> When economists calculate the GNP of our country, do you know that they don't even include the quality of air, the water and the soil? They call that externalities. Those are externalities to the considerations that we are making. Because they are limitless. They are free. Everybody has that. We can dump our crap into the air, the water, and soil. Nobody has to pay for that; that's shared by everyone else. What kind of economic system fails to account for the quality of the very life support systems in our country? (David Suzuki, Wabasca: 6053)

Would the Alpac project represent sustainable development? In its answer to this question, the company stated:

> Alberta-Pacific is committed to the use of environmentally sustainable economic development as a guiding principle for our future activities. Sustainable development is a

fledgling principle that requires concrete examples of success in the real world, before its true value can be understood. Alberta-Pacific looks forward to working with such groups as the Environmental Council of Alberta and the Sustainable Development Branch of Environment Canada to further our understanding of the phrase, and to guide us in its successful implementation.[57]

This statement indicates that the company believes that no one knows what sustainable development is in practice, only in theory. The company is committed to practising it—once the company and government departments determine what it is. The company thus both implicates government in its success or failure, and avoids the responsibility for being judged for sustainability before the project proceeds. The fact that its parent company, Crestbrook, failed the test is overlooked.

The one set of experimental data that we do have is areas in which you have already put in developments. Let's look at the history of this industry that is telling you that they are going to clean up their act. That is the best data that you have. Simon Lucas has just told you that seven or eight areas have been shut down around pulp mills in British Columbia to add to the two in Howe Sound that were shut down over a year ago. What is the history of this industry? . . . Look at the track record and look at the history. That is your data. Those are the hard facts that you have to judge and evaluate on. (David Suzuki, Wabasca: 6058-6059)

Also overlooked by the company's statement is the fact that there is insufficient baseline data against which to gauge whether the receiving environment can withstand the effects of the mill. The company thought studies could be conducted during the time the mill was being constructed and after:

[I]t is the feeling of our company that we can, in fact, provide enough information so that this project would be a viable one. And that the health studies, animal health studies, the studies on the effects of our emissions, will, in fact, substantiate that this mill is a viable project from an environmental position. (Gerry Fenner, Athabasca: 3074)

The Review Board was less sanguine about the advisability of giving the company a licence to construct in the absence of significant baseline information. Putting sustainability on the same footing as development would require doing fish studies and studies of existing levels of organochlorines in the Athabasca River system before approving the project, and this is what the Board recommended in its report.

Notes

1. All items identified as "Filed Documents" are written submissions to the Alpac EIA Review Board, a collection of the Filed Documents is housed in the Athabasca University Library; quotations from the Alberta-Pacific EIA Review Board public hearings are from J. G. Moore and Associates Ltd., *The Alberta-Pacific Environment Impact Assessment Review Board Public Hearing Proceedings, Volumes 1-55* (Edmonton, Alberta: J. G. Moore and Associates Ltd., 1989).

2. World Commission on Environment and Development, *Our Common Future* (Oxford: Oxford University Press, 1987), pp. 8-9.

3. William Rees, "Sustainable Development and the Biosphere: Concepts and Principles" (Paper presented to Teilhard Studies, 1990), p. 1.

4. William Rees, p. 1 (quoting from *Our Common Future*).

5. Hon. LeRoy Fjordbotten, Minister of Forestry, Lands and Wildlife, speaking to the estimates for his department. *Alberta Hansard,* 22nd Legislature, First Session, no. 45 (July 20, 1989): 905.

6. J. Stanley Rowe, "The Effects of Pulp Mills on the Environment" (Paper delivered at the Workshop on Bleached Kraft Pulp Mill Technology and Environmental Issues, Athabasca, Alberta, 1 March 1989), Alberta-Pacific Forest Industries Inc. *Environmental Impact Assessment. Bleached Kraft Mill Public Participation Program* (Edmonton, Alberta: Alberta-Pacific Forest Industries Inc., 1989), Appendix B, p. 98.

7. J. Stanley Rowe, p. 100.

8. "Proactive Government is Successful," *Programs, Activities and Initiatives* (Edmonton: Alberta Forestry, Lands and Wildlife, 1990), p. 3.

9. Andrew Nikiforuk and Ed Struzik, "The Great Forest Sell-off," *Toronto Globe and Mail, Report on Business Magazine* 6, no. 5 (November 1989): 57-68. Quotation from p. 63.

10. *Alberta Forest Development Opportunities* (Edmonton, Alberta: Alberta Forestry, Lands and Wildlife, 1989), p. 9.

11. F. W. McDougall, Deputy Minister, Forestry, Lands and Wildlife, Speech to Grande Prairie, Alberta, Chamber of Commerce, January 21, 1989.

12. LeRoy Fjordbotten, *Alberta Hansard* (July 18, 1989): 830.

13. LeRoy Fjordbotten, *Alberta Hansard* (June 15, 1989): 305.

14. *Major Forestry Projects.* Information Package for Departmental Staff for Public Involvement Sessions February-April 1989 (Edmonton, Alberta: Alberta Forestry, Lands and Wildlife, 1989), p. 35.

15. Frank Tester, "Reflections on Tin Wis: Environmentalism and the Evolution of Citizen Participation in Canada," *Alternatives: Perspectives*

on *Society, Technology and Environment* 19, no. 1 (October 1992): 34-41. Quotation from p. 39.

16. Joel Novek and Karen Kampen, "Sustainable or Unsustainable Development? An Analysis of an Environmental Controversy," *Canadian Journal of Sociology* 17, no. 3: 249-273.

17. Jeremy Seabrook, *The Myth of the Market: Promises and Illusions* (Montreal: Black Rose Press, 1991), p. 9.

18. *Athabasca Advertiser*, January 30, 1989.

19. Gerry Fenner, Athabasca: 2498.

20. Frank Tester, p. 40. Tester gives the example of the issue of killing dolphins in the process of fishing for tuna.

21. This and all further citations of the Alpac EIA Main Report in this chapter refer to Alberta-Pacific Forest Industries Inc., *Alberta-Pacific Forest Industries Inc. Environmental Impact Assessment. Bleached Kraft Pulp Mill Main Report* (Edmonton, Alberta: Alberta-Pacific Forest Industries Inc., 1989).

22. The Alberta Government Presentation on the Report of the EIA Review Board on The Proposed Alberta-Pacific Pulp Mill, Athabasca Community Centre, Athabasca, Alberta, March 2, 1990, p. 13.

23. Charles Beaver, Wabasca: 6039.

24. Charles Beaver, Wabasca: 6040.

25. The Alberta Government Presentation, p. 14.

26. Gerry Fenner, Edmonton: 4682-4683.

27. Alberta-Pacific Environmental Impact Assessment Review Board, *The Proposed Alberta-Pacific Pulp Mill: Report of the EIA Review Board* (Edmonton, Alberta: Alberta Environment, 1990), pp. 52-54.

28. Andrew Nikiforuk and Ed Struzik, p. 67.

29. Barry Johnstone and Mike Gismondi, "A Forestry Boom in Alberta?" *Probe Post* 12, no. 1 (Spring 1989): 16-19. Quotation from p. 17.

30. Alpac EIA Main Report, p. 1.3.

31. John McInnis, *Alberta Hansard* (June 21, 1989): 435.

32. LeRoy Fjordbotten, *Alberta Hansard* (July 18, 1989): 830.

33. Anita Gordon and David Suzuki, *It's a Matter of Survival* (Toronto: Stoddart, 1990), p. 154.

34. Alberta-Pacific Forest Industries Inc., *Alberta-Pacific Forest Industries Inc. Written Submissions and Responses Volumes 1, 2 and 3* (Edmonton, Alberta: Alberta-Pacific Forest Industries Inc., 1989), Item: Corporate Citizen, p. 149.

35. Herman E. Daly and John B. Cobb, Jr., For the Common Good: Redirecting the Economy Toward Community, the Environment and a Sustainable Future (Boston: Beacon Press, 1989), p. 83.

36. William Rees, p. 7.

37. Alberta-Pacific Forest Industries Inc. Final Document Submission: List of Undertakings in answer to the question Section 8.1 "Will Alberta-Pacific meet the principles of sustainable development?"

"[A]n animal may be debilitated and essentially ecologically dead by
conditions below those which kill it."
(Ian Birtwell, federal Department of Fisheries
and Oceans, Athabasca: 2799)
(Cartoon by Malcolm Mayes. Reprinted with permission of
The Edmonton Journal)

CHAPTER 4

Talking About Science in a Public Forum

Beak Associates [the consultants who prepared Alpac's EIA Main Report] are like the dating services in the yellow pages– they'll do anything to please a client. (Joseph Cummins)[1]

Alberta-Pacific is committed to ensuring that the local and regional environmental impacts of the pulp mill are minimized, and to this end has incorporated state-of-the-art environmental control technology in the process design. (Alpac EIA Main Report: Section 3.0, p. 3.1)[2]

We cannot afford any more of the obfuscational rhetoric with which industry and government try to evade reality and truth with stupid, meaningless phrases like "leading edge technology." (Kristin Reed, Fort McMurray: 555)[3]

The purpose of environmental impact assessment is to predict the effects of large industrial projects or other deliberate human actions, such as the building of dams, on the environment. To be done well, environmental impact assessment requires a good deal of knowledge of what the environment is, how it functions, and how its functioning will be affected by the activity in question. Fred Roots asks, "If science is organized knowledge of any kind . . . what kinds of science are needed for environmental impact assessment in the modern context?" He answers the question this way:

> In almost every case it will be found that the range and depth
> of science is different, and usually broader, than that required
> by the activity being assessed, simply to carry out its own

operations to achieve its primary goals. This is an important reason why the proponents of an activity often find that the business of environmental impact assessment is an expense, a nuisance, and a distraction which may, if imposed too late, defeat the original project.[4]

For example, one question that had to be addressed in Alpac's EIA was the effect of the proposed project on the Athabasca River and on fish downstream from the mill. In order to assess this impact, one would need to consider many things—existing water quality, existing fish stocks and spawning areas, what levels of what pollutants could be expected to flow into the river, how they would be carried downstream, the effects they would have on fish, and so on.

Corporations usually employ consulting firms to write their environmental impact assessment documents. Typically these firms do little original research; instead, they gather existing information, data, and theories by doing such things as conducting literature searches and interviewing industry officials. On the basis of information gathered, the consultants make predictions about the effects of the projects. Impact science could be done differently; for example, original research could be done to fill information gaps. Alpac's EIA involved some data collection, but relied for the most part on existing information.

When members of the public questioned the quality of "impact science" in Alpac's EIA, they used many of the same criteria they would use to judge any scientific publication: were the data sufficient to support the predictions, or were the "predictions" in fact guesses or fond hopes; was all of the available data considered, and given appropriate weight; how was conflicting data handled; does data gathered in one location apply to other locations; was scientific uncertainty acknowledged. Thus, when the quality of impact science was questioned, it was usually because it was thought not to measure up to rigorous scientific standards. Some questions were also raised about whether certain scientific methods and assumptions were suitable for impact science.

Participants in the Alpac hearing process called into question the quantity and quality of evidence in the documents; presented testimony from counter-experts, that is, experts who disagreed with the company-paid experts; and argued that impact science must be complemented by traditional knowledge possessed by native people. Furthermore, public participants seriously questioned the assumption that science, or at least impact science, is value-free or above political manipulation.

This chapter examines four criticisms of the science in Alpac's EIA raised at the public hearings: the company's misleading claims about the production of dioxin in the process of bleaching pulp with chlorine; its use of the LC50 toxicity test; its failure to meet the standards required for publishing in scientific journals; and its failure to incorporate native traditional knowledge. Debates about these issues were not just exercises in hairsplitting or language games—they could have important consequences. If the scientific findings suggested that the mill would fail to meet certain environmental standards, or would breach existing regulations (such as those governing human health or fisheries), the proposal would be in jeopardy.

Explaining Chlorine Bleaching and Dioxin to Lay People

The most toxic of dioxins, 2,3,7,8-TCDD . . . is widely reputed to be the most toxic substance ever manufactured. (Review Board Report: 22)[5]

One particular chlorinated organic compound "dioxin" (2,3,7,8-tetrachlorodibenzo-p-dioxin), which has been a major public concern, can now be reduced to levels which, it is anticipated, will be below the limits of detection. . . . However even if "dioxin" could be detected . . . there is no good evidence that it would constitute a human health problem. No deaths in humans, due to "dioxin," have been documented to date. This does not mean that "dioxin" is not an environmental concern in other situations . . . although the extent of its toxicity to man has not been defined, it has probably been greatly exaggerated. (Alpac Health Report)[6]

The Alpac EIA stated that "the risks associated with chlorine and chlorine discharge were clearly of significant public concern and were raised in virtually every meeting held between Alberta-Pacific personnel and area communities."[7] Organochlorines, including dioxins and furans, are by-products of the pulp bleaching process:

The source of these compounds and most other organo-chlorines was discovered to be the chlorine bleaching process, where high concentrations of lignin and other organic materials dissolved from wood fibre are exposed to high concentrations of chlorine. (Review Board Report: 21)

While specialists at some of the technical hearing sessions addressed the causes and fate of these toxins, at most hearings complex scientific questions, among them the issue of dioxins, were simplified to aid public understanding. The EIA document itself was "designed to have an easily understood main report followed by technical appendices containing more detailed information."[8] However, the process of simplifying issues for lay understanding was not always innocent. In addressing chlorine bleaching and the public fear of dioxins, Alpac's Gerry Fenner, speaking at an EIA meeting in Athabasca, explained that:

{C]hlorine is one of the elements of salt, basic household table salt. If you took household salt, put it in a jar, stirred it up with water and stuck an electrode in it, you would get chlorine and caustic. Chlorine and caustic are the two chemicals we use in the bleaching process.[9]

By comparing table salt and a familiar elementary school science project to the main ingredients and the process of bleaching kraft pulp, Fenner made toxic dioxins and furans either "disappear" altogether, or appear harmless, like ordinary table salt.

Fenner's presentation of science to the lay person was an effort to downplay the dangers of bleaching pulp with chlorine. As was pointed out at the hearings, similar techniques have been recommended by the American Paper Institute:

When the American Paper Institute [API] realized they had a serious problem on their hands, i.e., the creation of dioxin as a by-product, the API went to great lengths to lobby congressmen and senators and civil servants within the US environmental protection agencies. A public relations firm was hired to create "kits" and "press releases" for pulp mill companies to use to downplay dioxin to the media, the local government and the public.

The overall objective of this PR campaign was to: "Keep allegations of health risks out of public arena—or minimize them; and avoid confrontations with government agencies which might trigger concerns about health risks or raise visibility of the issue generally." (Joan Sherman, Filed Document G-42: 11)

The American Paper Institute directed its members—the pulp industry—both to downplay public concerns about dioxin, and to make public statements, such as "dioxin detected at some pulp and paper mills is in extremely low quantities—levels not even measurable as recently as two years ago."[10] Alpac's technical consultant on health issues, J. D. Taylor, used the phrase "below the limits of detection"[11] to suggest that Alpac's fibre line would not produce enough dioxin to cause harm.

The company's technical consultant on dioxins, Bruce Fleming, of the Pulp and Paper Research Institute of Canada, used the same ploy in discussing a graph showing how dioxin production was reduced with an increase in the use of chlorine dioxide (instead of elemental chlorine) in the bleaching process:

> What this plot shows is that for mills operating at high chlorine multiples and also low chlorine dioxide substitution—and that's where most of the Canadian mills were with those red spots two years ago, they were in the dioxin zone—and if they can either decrease their chlorine multiple or increase their chlorine dioxide substitution, they can come into the safe zone where the dioxins will be non-detectable. (Bruce Fleming, Edmonton: 5973)

In calling the part of the graph in which detectable amounts of dioxin are produced the "dioxin zone" and the part of the graph in which non-detectable amounts of dioxin are produced the "safe zone," Fleming begged the question of whether "non-detectable" amounts of dioxin are safe.[12] The Review Board reported, however, that:

> Information was presented . . . that dioxins and furans at very low, even undetectable concentrations in water had been concentrated in organisms enough to cause reproductive failure in predatory fishes such as rainbow trout, and in fish-eating birds such as herons, gulls, terns and cormorants, due to biomagnification in food chains. (Review Board Report: 23)

The LC50 Test and the Men Who Loved Fish

Evidence regarding sub-lethal impacts on fish (e.g., morbidity, growth impairment) in waters receiving treated bleached kraft mill effluent is inconclusive. Chronic toxicity is, in fact, often difficult to detect in non-laboratory conditions unless the effects are obvious. (Alpac EIA Main Report: Appendix 1, Section 3.2, p. 1.32)

Most of the effects that we are concerned about, both in fish and in human beings in terms of the Northwest Territories, are those effects which we would call sub-lethal or that they are delayed, and that they are not acute in the sense that they happen very quickly as a result of let's say, a test undertaken on fish swimming in effluent near the plant. (Peter Sly, Fort Smith: 2008)

Alpac planned to draw water from the Athabasca River to use in the pulping process. Waste-water, or effluent, created in the pulp-digestion and bleaching stages would be collected in sewers and directed to a biological effluent treatment system in large holding ponds. Although treated, the effluent would contain certain amounts of pollutants when returned to the river. The company contended that the quality of the effluent would be monitored, and that it should be non-toxic to fish and other aquatic organisms.

Scientists speak of two types of toxic effects of pulp-mill effluent: lethal, that is, effects which cause death; and sub-lethal, that is, effects which are debilitating in various ways, but do not kill the organism outright. Each type of toxic effect can occur over the short term or the long term. Short-term lethal toxicity is measured by the LC50 (lethal concentration 50%) test. "Samples of effluent identified as 'non-toxic' are those in which more than half (50%) of the test fish exposed to full-strength effluent for 96 hours survived."[8] In other words, if Alpac's undiluted pulp-mill effluent were to kill slightly less than 50 per cent of the test fish within 96 hours, the effluent would pass the test. In Alberta, licence conditions for existing kraft mills include quarterly testing of undiluted effluent by the LC50 test. Alpac's data suggested that its effluent, unlike that of many mills in Ontario and British Columbia, would routinely pass this test, and that claim was not disputed.

To this point in the review, the LC50 test was described in such neutral terms that it was hard to form a picture of what the test involved—people putting fish into buckets of effluent and coming back in 96 hours to see how many of them survived.[4] The unadulterated dullness of the scientists' testimony was much like that of a coroner at a murder trial:

> Most of the existing information we have about aquatic toxicity of specific constituents of pulp mill effluents has been determined from acute lethal toxicity testing. We expose the [test species] to effluent solutions and examine lethality or death; the net result of that is we get a number called the 96 hour LC50 which is the concentration which causes mortality in 50% of the test species over a 96 hour period. (Ron Voss, Alpac Technical Workshop)[5]

However, when Lyle Lockhart and Ian Birtwell, of the federal Department of Fisheries and Oceans, began to discuss research on biological effects of pulp-mill effluent on fish, they altered the discourse dramatically:

> Lockhart: I want to talk for a few minutes now on biological effects. We know that if it [dioxin] gets into the water or the sediment or the food, it will occur in the fish. It may or may not build up to an amount which makes the fish objectionable as food, but I think as a Fisheries Department, we are also concerned about what it might do to the fish. (Athabasca: 2651-2652)

> Birtwell: My main area of research is on the sub-lethal effects of contaminants, that is, levels that don't inherently kill fish outright, but perhaps may have an effect at a level below that that would have killed them. . . . [M]any times an animal may be debilitated and essentially ecologically dead by conditions far below those which kill it in four days, and kill 50 per cent of them in four days. Surely what we are trying to do is protect that level of population, the zero to 50 per cent that is sensitive. (Athabasca: 2799-2801)

Here Birtwell questioned the LC50 test as a way of determining whether pulp-mill effluent is toxic to fish. In fact, he suggested that while Alpac's effluent would pass the test, this "success" did not indicate that the effluent would be harmless or of low risk to fish. Hence, he cast some doubt on the underlying assumptions of the LC50 test, and on the positive impression that passing it made on the public.

Similarly, Lockhart's presentation on long-term sub-lethal effects on fish, such as tumours, lesions, growth impairment, and changes in liver and reproductive functioning, focused attention on the area in which Alpac had admitted its evidence was inconclusive.

On the basis of the presentations by Lockhart, Birtwell, and other members of the Department of Fisheries and Oceans, the Review Board recommended that studies be done on fish in the Athabasca-Peace-Slave river system to determine "whether concentrations of organochlorine compounds are stable, and whether the fish and other aquatic life are, and will remain, unimpaired and safe for human consumption."[16]

Birtwell's discourse on the relevance of the health of the surviving fish did more than question the value of the LC50 test. His love of fish revealed a subjective aspect of science that was stunning after months of dry discussions of whether the mill's effluent would pass the LC50 test. His discourse broke free from two widely held assumptions about scientific practice and writing. One is that although it may be acceptable, or even a good thing, to have emotional responses to animals as a person, as a scientist, one must maintain objectivity, that is, treat animals strictly as objects of study. Scientific language becomes more abstract the more the scientist objectifies the organism under study—to the extent that what is studied is "lethality" and "death" rather than fish dying because people had immersed them in poison. To this point in the review, if members of the public expressed attachment to the environment, or a part of it that they thought might be harmed by the project, their testimony was discounted by the proponent as emotional, and thus non-scientific and irrelevant to the matter at hand. In fact, a standard way of deflecting criticism was to say that critics were just being emotional. When Alpac showed a human face, however, it enhanced its position, because it was careful to show that the very technicians who were so knowledgeable and objective about the details of the mill and its operations were "people too." For example, after hours of responses based on technical details, Alpac's Vice President Pulp, Gerry Fenner, reminded parents concerned about their children's health that he, too, was a parent, that he fished with his kids downstream from the pulp mill he managed in Skookumchuk, BC, and that they enjoyed eating those fish. Lockhart and Birtwell altered the discourse when they reminded listeners that fish are subjects in their own right, organisms that can suffer harm, and when they stated that they were concerned, as scientists, about protecting fish.

The testimony of Lockhart and Birtwell also questioned the assumption that scientific statements express facts or theories, not values. In questioning the assumptions behind the LC50 test, Birtwell revealed that in devising toxicity tests, scientists make value judgements about what constitutes harm to organisms.[17]

Is Impact Science Good Science?[B]

> Brian Bietz (Beak Associates representative): An EIA . . . unfortunately or fortunately . . . requires a lot of professional opinion . . . therefore while one would have loved to achieve the rigours of a thesis. . . my experience has been that eventually we as biologists have to be willing to make predictions based on available data . . . if we wring our hands and simply say we don't have enough information . . . the projects go ahead without our input.
>
> Therefore I would challenge your basic premise that it is a thesis, it has never been designed as that . . . An EIA is designed as a best prediction based on opinions not only of myself but of a number of people . . . as to what the changes would be to the environment, we don't claim prescience, we don't claim to be perfect, we do offer it up, though, for peer review.
>
> Bill Fuller (Athabasca area resident): I didn't mean to imply that it would have the same rigour as a thesis, what I meant . . . is that it is an important document, in the real world it is more important than many theses that are based on small, esoteric bits of science. My question really is: Is it science or is it not. Is this a scientific document? . . . Or, is it a document based on the examination of the entrails of a chicken?[D]

Bill Fuller, a member of the Friends of the Athabasca Environmental Association, discussed the quality of the science in the Alpac EIA in his presentation to the Review Board. Fuller, Professor Emeritus and former Chair of the Department of Zoology at the University of Alberta, had participated as a member of two federal environmental assessment review panels. He had worked for years in the Peace-Athabasca delta, and he chose to retire near Athabasca to be close to a northern river. Fuller prefaced his presentation to the Review Board with a question:

What in all the mass of material submitted by . . . Alpac . . . what in all of the hundreds of pages that I read would be accepted for publication and in a peer review journal if it was submitted to me for refereeing? The only answer I can come up with is nothing, zero, zilch, dick all, however you want to express it. (Athabasca: 2950-2951)

Now these feelings could easily be dismissed as the words of a crusty scientist who was bitter about losing his retirement paradise, but Fuller next read from an editorial, titled "Impact Statement Boondoggle," that appeared in the May 7, 1976, issue of *Science*:

Many politicians have been quick to grasp that the quickest way to silence critical "eco-freaks" is to allocate a small proportion of funds to any engineering project for ecological studies. Someone is inevitably available to receive these funds, conduct the studies, regardless of how quickly results are demanded, write large reports containing reams of un-interpreted and incomplete descriptive data and, in some cases, construct "predictive" models irrespective of the quality of the data base. These reports have formed a "gray literature" of reports . . . voluminous and so limited in distribution that its conclusions and recommendations are never scrutinized. . . . Often the author's only scientific credentials are the impressive title in a government agency, university or consulting firm. This title, the mass of the report, the author's salary, and his dress and bearing often carry more weight with the commission or study board, to whom the statement is presented, than either his scientific competence or the validity of his scientific investigation. Indeed, many agencies have found it in their best interests to employ a "travelling circus" of "scientists" with credentials matching those requirements. As a result, impact statements seldom receive the hard scrutiny that follows the publication of scientific findings in a reputable scientific journal. (Quoted by Fuller, Athabasca: 2951-2952)

Here we have Fuller the scientist, sitting in front of two scientists on the Review Board, facing five or six Alpac-employed scientists across the room, uttering this devastating critique of impact science into the record. The author of this editorial was the scientist Alpac feared the most—none other than Review Board member Dr. David Schindler. By quoting Schindler's critique in his presentation, Fuller used the situation of the discourse to empower his efforts to draw attention to the poor quality of the science in Alpac's EIA.

An important transition occurred here. Throughout the year of the Alpac open houses and public presentations, mill boosters often abdicated review of the science in the EIA, either to the proponent ("we trust Alpac") or to the government ("we trust our civil servants"). Scientists belonging to environmental groups were less inclined to abdicate this responsibility; and as lay people read and re-read the EIA documentation, they too began to criticize the science or social science in the proposal, and often asked for independent verification of company studies, or for further studies that Alpac had felt were unnecessary. By successfully questioning the quality of the science in Alpac's EIA, Fuller helped to legitimate the doubts of other scientists and of non-scientist citizens.

In his editorial, Schindler had not only characterized impact science as underfunded, subjected to unreasonably short timelines, carried out by people who might not be qualified, exempt from peer review, and prone to make predictions on the basis of inadequate data, but also made the political point that governments appropriate the rhetoric, but not the substance, of good science to silence opposition.

Fuller took the point one step further. Within the theatre of the hearing, he prepared his dramatic conclusion. After arguing that science in general was more rigorous than the impact science in Alpac's EIA, Fuller contended that impact science, which may be used to make decisions that will affect the environment, should be even more rigorous than ordinary science, which may have no application outside the laboratory. Reading from another Schindler letter that appeared in the July 16, 1976, issue of *Science*, Fuller concluded:

[S]cience is a self-correcting endeavour . . . "and one is confident that correct results will always come eventually, leaving only a relatively harmless pile of worthless papers, wasted manhours, and broken test tubes behind. But we cannot afford to let impact science follow tradition. The legacy will not be broken test tubes, but hopelessly and permanently crippled ecosystems." (Quoted by Fuller, Athabasca: 2952-2953)

In challenging the quality of the science underpinning Alpac's predictive claims, critics such as Fuller and Schindler did not address the shortcomings of science. Rather, they championed science and showed that impact science fell short. Other participants observed that a shortcoming of science itself was its failure to incorporate traditional native knowledge.

Native or Traditional Knowledge

[T]he Indian person who speaks or tells you about whatever is going to happen, his word versus these specialized white people, the scientists, the environmentalist, their words are more solid, they are more powerful than the Indian speaking. (Sal Marten, Elder, Fort Chipewyan: 1348)

Although debate on the issue of traditional native knowledge was limited at the public hearings, and was not reflected in the Review Board's report, it was agreed that scientists should consult native people to fill information gaps about wildlife species, numbers and locations. Points were also raised about the methods natives use to make predictions, and about assumptions that lie behind their thinking about environmental impacts.

In the same year as the Alpac hearings were held, a series of controversies involving native people and environmental issues burst on the Canadian scene at both the provincial and the national levels. For example, the massive James Bay hydro-electric projects threatened native communities in northern Quebec; low-level military flights threatened the Innu of Labrador; clearcut logging in northern Ontario continued to threaten natives' traditional life-styles and lands; uranium mining in Saskatchewan threatened natives' health; the shellfish industry off Howe Sound, British Columbia, was closed because of dioxin and furan contamination from pulp-mill effluent; and logging threatened native traditions on South Moresby Island. In Alberta, the Peigans resisted the damming of the Oldman River, and the Lubicon escalated their struggles for a land claim settlement when the Daishowa pulp mill planned to begin logging on traditional Lubicon lands. In each of these cases, natives reported that serious environmental and social impacts occurred, despite assurances to the contrary from government and industry experts and scientists. It was in this context that some natives expressed concern about the status accorded to scientists, and the lack of appreciation shown for the knowledge that native people bring to environmental impact assessment.

Part of the reason science enjoys a high status in western society is its purported reliance on a rational methodology, which is thought to place it above personality, prejudice, and ethnocentrism. Review Board member Cindy Gilday, a native from the Northwest Territories, challenged this belief, however, when she questioned whether western science had a place in it for native traditional knowledge:

> Gilday: . . . you said that the rigorous academic level should be applied to the EIA process as it is in regular science practices. . . . Native people . . . have worked very hard to have the scientists acknowledge traditional management of animals and lands and waters and all those things. Does this requirement include the traditional knowledge as well?

> Fuller: Well, certainly the traditional knowledge is valuable. I didn't mean that traditional knowledge shouldn't be used. But in terms of evaluating the river quality, I'm not sure that the traditional knowledge is able to do the analyses for these organochlorines. That is the sort of thing I meant. Not to leave out any source of information, but the study must be done rigorously enough, complete enough that it meets all the standards for scientific publication.

> Gilday: My understanding is a lot of species of fish are missed by biologists simply because they never bothered to ask the Indian people who know the land because of the language factor. . . . But it's been a very long fight by Indian people in the world to have their traditional knowledge acknowledged by the scientific community. I think if you are going to do a proper EIA that pertains to Native people, then this factor has to be included in the scientific academic rigours of science. (Athabasca: 2956-2957)

Some scientists do consider augmenting scientific data with information based on traditional knowledge of habitat, species variety, life cycle patterns, and so on.[20] But gaining information is one thing, and interpreting it is another. According to Martha Johnson, Director of Research with the Dene Cultural Institute in Yellowknife, NWT:

[T]he main difference between the two knowledge systems [western science and traditional knowledge] appears to be . . . western scientists stress the use of quantitative measures, while the traditional Dene harvester is more concerned with qualitative information . . . more concerned with conditions in general (e.g., species scarce or plentiful for his use) or in trends (e.g., increasing or decreasing) than he is in precise numbers and averages.[21]

Can qualitative information provided by native people be used in environmental impact assessment? Ron Wallace, speaking for the Athabasca Tribal Council, suggested at the hearings that qualitative evidence might be used to provide baseline data about fisheries and river conditions. This evidence would be helpful because the absence of baseline data for long reaches of the Athabasca River was of concern to the Review Board:

[I]t was felt by a number of scientists that people's recollections of water quality, especially those individuals who were close to the resource, could be an extremely valuable indicator of change. . . . [T]he reason I feel this is a valuable reflection of scientific indications of the quality of the water is, one, we don't have any hard data; and two, these people, whenever tested, have in fact produced astonishingly accurate qualitative reflections of water quality problems. . . . [Q]ualitative impressions by the Natives have been fully vindicated in the last three years by scientific studies done by teams of scientists. . . . What this did for me was it established the necessity to listen closely to the users of this resource as very valuable indicators, qualitative indicators of change in these ecosystems. (Ron Wallace, Fort Chipewyan: 1578-1579)

Here, Wallace was trying to convince the Review Board of the validity of native people's non-quantitative information. It was politically astute of him to validate these qualitative findings as substantiated by scientists, because as Elder Sal Marten had said, "their words are more solid, they are more powerful than the Indian speaking."

However, although the words of white scientists may be more powerful politically, Dene speaker Gerry Cheezie offered a native perspective on risk that brought the discussion back to the assumptions that lie behind environmental impact assessment. Cheezie spoke in terms of survival in a hard climate, not of balancing environmental degradation against economic development, and reminded listeners that even after all the data are in, value judgements must still be made about what is safe and what is too risky.

> We look at the situation in this way. If a person catches a fish and the fish looks unhealthy, they won't eat it. We don't take those chances. This comes from centuries of survival on the land. People who take chances end up hurting themselves. You have to be careful. Well, here are some fish. They have low levels of some chemicals that are dangerous. Scientists can't say if the fish are safe to eat, so we don't eat them. Then someone comes along and says they want to add more poison to the fish. It doesn't take a whole lot of thought to know what a careful person would say. (Gerry Cheezie, Dene Nation, Fort Resolution: 3695)

In the next chapter, we continue to explore the concerns raised by native people at the hearings by considering the issues of special populations at risk, and ethnocentrism in scientific standards.

Notes
1. Dr. Joseph Cummins speaking in Athabasca. Photo caption. *The Athabaskan*, February 20, 1989, p. 1.
2. This and all further citations of the Alpac EIA Main Report in this chapter refer to Alberta-Pacific Forest Industries Inc., *Alberta-Pacific Forest Industries Inc. Environmental Impact Assessment. Bleached Kraft Pulp Mill Main Report* (Edmonton, Alberta: Alberta-Pacific Forest Industries Inc., 1989).
3. All items identified as "Filed Documents" are written submissions to the Alpac EIA Review Board, a collection of the Filed Documents is housed in the Athabasca University Library; quotations from the Alberta-Pacific EIA Review Board public hearings are from J. G. Moore and Associates Ltd., *The Alberta-Pacific Environment Impact Assessment Review Board Public Hearing Proceedings, Volumes 1-55* (Edmonton, Alberta: J. G. Moore and Associates Ltd., 1989).
4. E. F. Roots, "Some Concepts and Issues Surrounding the Place of Science in Assessment of Impacts on the Environment," Workshop Presentation for "The Role of Science in Environmental Impact Assessment," Edmonton, April, 1992, p. 3.

5. This and all further citations of the Review Board Report in this chapter refer to Alberta-Pacific Environmental Impact Assessment Review Board, *The Proposed Alberta-Pacific Pulp Mill: Report of the EIA Review Board,* March 1990 (Edmonton, Alberta: Alberta Environment, 1990).

6. J. D. Taylor, Ph.D., *Environmental Health Issues Associated with A Modern Bleached Kraft Pulp Mill* (Edmonton, Alberta: Alberta-Pacific Forest Industries Inc., 1989), pp. 2-3.

7. Alpac EIA Main Report, Section 4.1.3.5: 4.7.

8. Alpac EIA Main Report, Section 1.3: 1.5.

9. Alberta-Pacific Vice President Pulp, Gerry Fenner, speaking at an Athabasca EIA meeting, June 2, 1989. Videotape.

10. Joan Sherman, Athabasca. Public Hearing Filed Document G-42: 11. The material quoted is from Letter and Enclosure to Ms. Susan Ford from Carol L. Raulsten, American Paper Institute, March 18, 1987.

11. J. D. Taylor, p. 2.

12. See the discussion of scientific uncertainty and environmental ethics in Donald A. Brown, "The Most Important Problem for Environmental Ethics: The Failure to Integrate Environmental Ethics Into Daily Environmental Decision Making," International Forum for Biophilosophy, *Stability and Change in Nature: Ecological And Cultural Dimensions,* Proceedings of the IFB Conference, Budapest, Hungary, March 1992, p. 8; for discussions of political influences on scientific knowledge, methods, and reporting, see Patti Lather, *Feminist Research in Education: Within/Against* (Geelong, Victoria, Australia: Deakin University, 1991), pp. 12, 14; Stanley Aronowitz, *Science as Power: Discourse and Ideology in Modern Society* (Minneapolis: University of Minnesota Press, 1988); Bruno Latour, *Science in Action: How to Follow Scientists and Engineers through Society* (Cambridge: Harvard University Press, 1987); G. Nigel Gilbert and Michael Mulkay, *Opening Pandora's Box: A Sociological Analysis of Scientists' Discourse* (Cambridge: Cambridge University Press, 1984).

13. Environment Canada, *Aquatic Toxicity of Pulp and Paper Mill Effluent: A Review* (Ottawa: Minister of Supply and Services, 1987), p. 36.

14. See the discussion of scientific discourse in Roger Anderson, *The Power and the Word: Language, Power and Change* (London: Paladin Grafton Books, 1988); M. Jimmie Killingsworth and Dean Steffens, "Effectiveness in the Environmental Impact Statement: A Study in Public Rhetoric," *Written Communication* 6, no. 2 (1989): 159.

15 Ron H. Voss, "Trace Organic Contaminants in Pulp Mill Effluents and their Environmental Effects," in *Alberta-Pacific Forest Industries Inc. Environmental Impact Assessment: Bleached Kraft Mill Public Participation Program, Appendix B: Technical Workshop Proceedings,* p. 68.

16. Review Board Report: 32.

17. See, for example, Robert N. Proctor, *Value Free Science?: Purity and Power in Modern Knowledge* (Cambridge: Harvard University Press, 1991); Donald A. Brown, *Op. cit.;* Conrad Brunk, Lawrence Haworth, and Brenda Lee, *Value Assumptions in Risk Assessment: A Case Study of the Alachlor Controversy* (Waterloo: Wilfrid Laurier University Press, 1991).

18. An earlier version of this section appears in Michael Gismondi and Mary Richardson, "Discourse and Power in Environmental Politics: Public Hearings on a Bleached Kraft Pulp Mill in Alberta, Canada," *Capitalism Nature Socialism* 2, no. 8 (October 1991): 43-66.

19. Part of an exchange between Brian Bietz of Beak Consultants, authors of the Alpac EIA Report, and Dr. Bill Fuller at an EIA meeting in Athabasca, June 2, 1989. Videotape.

20. Douglas J. Nakashima, *Application of Native Knowledge in EIA: Inuit, Eiders and Hudson Bay Oil* (Ottawa: Minister of Supply and Services, 1990).

21. Martha Johnson, "Dene Traditional Knowledge," *Northern Perspectives* 20, no. 1 (Summer 1992): 3-5. Quotation from p. 3. See also Milton R. Freeman, "The Nature and Utility of Traditional Ecological Knowledge," *Northern Perspectives* 20, no. 1: 9-12.

"[W]e have forgotten the aboriginal philosophy which states that when
making any major decisions, we should look ahead at least seven
generations. . . ."
(Geraldine Manossa, Athabasca: 3127)
(Photograph courtesy of Alberta Environmental Protection)

CHAPTER 5

Ethnocentrism in Scientific Standards[1]

Bioaccumulation of such chlorinated organic compounds [i.e. those found in biologically treated kraft mill effluent], if it occurs, is usually in the livers of fish, not the muscle tissue. Thus the likelihood that these compounds will be ingested by people through fish consumption is slight. (Alpac EIA Main Report: Appendix 1, p. 1-2.35)[2]

Alberta-Pacific's EIA says that dioxins and other chlorinated organics accumulate in the fatty tissues of fish and in fish livers. The EIA goes on to say that human ingestion of chlorinated organics would be slight because people don't eat fish liver. Well, people in our region do eat fish liver. In fact, loche or burbot liver is considered a delicacy. (Frank Pope, for the Shihta Regional Council, Edmonton: 5376)[3]

In this chapter, we explore the concern raised at the Alpac public hearings about the potential negative effects on the health of native Canadians resulting from eating fish, especially fish liver, contaminated with dioxin and furan from pulp-mill effluent. The concern is based on the fact that the Canadian government did not take the fish consumption patterns of natives into account when it set health standards for dioxin and furan concentrations in fish.

During the hearings for the Alpac mill, there was a great deal of debate between government and industry scientists about the downstream effects of pulp-mill effluents. The debate started as a scientific argument over the presence or absence of dioxins and furans in the mill effluent, and about the toxicity of these substances.

The terms of the debate changed significantly, however, when the concept of "special populations at risk" was introduced, and it was suggested by the Review Board member from the Northwest Territories that Canadian health standards for fish consumption are ethnocentric, because they are based on the assumption that the average Canadian eats relatively little fish, whereas fish is a dietary staple for many native Canadians.

Country Food and Special Populations at Risk

> We repeat: We have been unable to find any evidence linking effluents from other pulp mills with human health problems, and therefore we have no reason to believe that downstream users' health will be affected by effluents from the Alberta-Pacific mill. We assume, or predict, if you will, that downstream users' health will not be affected. This is an entirely reasonable assumption—just like your assumption that your well water is safe to drink because you have no evidence that it isn't. (Alpac Written Responses)[4]

> Some participants stated that there was no direct evidence that dioxins or furans were harmful to humans. However, no reference was made in these presentations to studies on humans done in the past three years. The scarcity of direct evidence of harm to humans may be due to the fact that there are no controlled long-term experiments using humans, and few long-term epidemiological studies. . . . [T]wo scientific studies published in late 1989 . . . indicate that dioxin exposure has caused increased cancer rates at several sites in humans, and a recently-published study [links] increased cancers of the digestive tract and lymph system in pulp and paper workers to organochlorine exposure. . . . Due to the high fish consumption by northern Aboriginal Peoples, and in particular their consumption of burbot livers, total organochlorine contamination of the Slave River from all sources is of concern to the Board. (Review Board Report: 22, 28)[5]

Two of the most toxic pollutants in pulp-mill effluent were the focus of the Review Board's concern: 2,3,7,8-TCDD dioxin and 2,3,7,8-TCDF furan. These substances were already produced in significant quantities in older bleached kraft pulp mills on the Peace-Athabasca river system, such as those in Hinton and Grande Prairie. 2,3,7,8-TCDD is reputed to be the most toxic substance ever produced.[6]

At the Review Board hearing in Edmonton, Jerome Slavik, lawyer for the Athabasca Tribal Council, asked representatives of Alberta Environment whether the department had:

[P]rior to setting permits and licence standards for previous pulp mills, examined in-depth the impact of organic chlorides, including dioxins and furans, on the health of the fishery and the human users in the river. (Edmonton: 5936)

Referring to a newer kraft pulp mill on the Peace River approved just months before the Alpac review, Scott McClure replied on behalf of Alberta Environment:

We have only set one permit level. It was for total organic chlorides on the Daishowa permit to construct. . . . We did not undertake any impact studies, that I know of, at that time. We were basing the standard then on what we thought was the technology's capabilities. (Edmonton: 5937)

This testimony was worrisome, because it suggested that the limits of technology, not health considerations, determined effluent regulations of bleached kraft pulp mills in Alberta. As Slavik concluded:

[I]n setting AOX, dioxin or furan standards in the licences . . . Alberta Environment, in fact, does not consider the impacts and has no repertoire, research or inventory of the impacts of these materials on human health, and has not incorporated them into the factors of licensing the plants to date. (Edmonton: 5939)

Dioxins and furans are not easily broken down in nature; hence, they persist in ecosystems. They bioaccumulate and bio-magnify in foodchains and may reach high concentrations in fish livers and fatty tissues. They are also adsorbed onto river sediments; in northern Alberta, river sediments are carried down the Athabasca and Peace rivers and deposited in the Peace-Athabasca delta or passed on to the Slave River Basin.

How dioxins and furans affect mammals up the food chain—including humans who eat fish—was hotly disputed during the hearings. Alpac brought toxicologists to argue for "thresholds" (amounts of dioxin that could safely be ingested or taken up into human systems).[7] Others who testified thought the thresholds should be much lower than those established, or that it was not safe to ingest any amount of dioxin.[8]

A presentation by the Government of the Northwest Territories changed the frame of reference of this "dioxin threshold" discourse. The scientists who spoke on behalf of the NWT government raised the issue of a "special population at risk"—the native people of the NWT whose main source of protein is "country food."

Many hearing participants told the Review Board that the diet of native northerners consists largely of local fish and game. Northerners eat large amounts of fish, other aquatic animals and birds, and large and small game animals:

> The biggest part of the community use the fish for their main food resource. The muskrats is trapped, and the beaver, they are along the rivers. We use that for food. We use the waterfowl, the ducks, the geese that comes through here. That's all our food. The moose population is all food for the Native people in the community. So our community . . . that's all living on that wild food that is in the community. (Sonny Flett, Fort Chipewyan: 1467)

> The fish in the Slave, there is people . . . that fish there all summer and part of the winter. They are not only fishing for themselves, they sell it to anybody that wants to eat fish. . . . So it spreads throughout the community. And dogs, people use dogs, still use dogs. And they fish by the thousands of pounds in the fall so they can use it all winter. (Frank Laviolette, Fort Smith: 1948)

> Today, now, what I would like to say is that everything here, every living thing depends on water. The people drink water, the waterfowl drinks the water, the fish also drink the water. If they are going to damage the water what will the person eat . . . if all the wildlife is destroyed, what will the person eat . . . the people will also be affected by this water. (Mary Rose Waquan, Fort Chipewyan: 1351-1352)

Furthermore, natives in the Northwest Territories often eat animal organs, including fish liver, which contain higher concentrations of dioxin and furan than do muscle tissues. As Chief Bonnet Rouge of the Fort Providence Dene Band stated, "We would like to point out that contrary to the EIA, we do eat some organs, including the liver of animals, fish and birds."[9]

Evidence was presented at the hearings that:

> Health and Welfare Canada's . . . permissible concentrations of 2,3,7,8-TCDD in fish for human consumption . . . are based on assumed rates of fish consumption that are far lower than those of Aboriginal Peoples in the lower Athabasca, Slave and Mackenzie river systems. The rates of consumption assumed would allow a person weighing 70 kilograms to eat only an average of 35 grams (slightly more than one ounce) of fish per day. The Board was told that weekly consumption of fish by many Aboriginal Peoples of the above rivers may be more than 10-fold higher than that of average Canadians. (Review Board Report: 22-23)[10]

The following exchange clarifies the implications of this statement:

> Wayland Swain (Scientist for the NWT): The majority of the standards that have been developed . . . are based upon the average consumption pattern of the average human being . . . consuming something like between one and half and three and half grams of fish a day, or . . . something in the order of one fish meal per week for recreationally caught fish. (Edmonton: 5885)

> Bill Ross (Review Board member): . . perhaps I could just make sure I understand how . . . I might apply correction factors for these special populations. My assumption is that if a population eats, for example, 25 times more fish than the average New York resident, then I ought to reduce any standard by a factor of 25 to compensate for that; is that correct?

> Douglas Hallett (Scientist for the NWT): That's correct.

> Swain: [I]n fact, 25 is probably an extremely low number.

Cindy Gilday (Review Board member): [T]he kind of studies that you are talking about are very ethnocentric as far as the standards are concerned. We were in Fort Resolution where we were told, the man said that he eats fish five times a week. That's a father. And the mother also eats five fish a week. That's ten fish, one week, in one family's life. Considering what you told us this morning that we are not only talking about 10 parts of dioxin, but taking into consideration PCB and all the other compounds, when you look at it long term or cumulative impact, what would you say to the people in the Northwest Territories? What do they have to look forward to? (Edmonton: 5916-5917)

Gilday, a Slavey from Fort Franklin and the NWT representative on the Review Board, was the first to use the word "ethnocentrism"—the tendency to privilege (often unconsciously) the points of view of one's own cultural norms, values, and practices over those of another culture or society. The kind of ethnocentrism implicit and unrecognized in the Canadian government's health standards for fish is characterized by some sociologists as "institutional racism"—routine practices that discriminate against certain groups because they assume, for example, that all peoples and cultures relate to nature in the same way. As if to confirm the presence of this form of racism, it was the Government of the Northwest Territories, which has many elected officials who are from the First Nations of Canada, and who represent a large number of native people, that brought Swain and Hallett to testify against the governments of Canada and Alberta, and the project proponent.

It should be noted that in toxicological studies, it is "not the mean [fish] consumption, but rather the upper extremes of consumption which are the focus of concern."[11] The debate about fish consumption in the Alpac hearings focused on average native consumers, not those who ate extremely large amounts of fish and other aquatic animals, or large amounts of fish liver. That is, they did not deal with those most at risk within a population at risk. As Jack Vallentyne, testifying for the Athabasca Tribal Council, noted:

Most calculations of risk disregard uncertainties, particularly for populations at special risk. The very young, the very old and the health impaired are seldom taken into account in calculations of risk. The important question is: Whose health are we not protecting? (Edmonton: 4916-4917)

Intergenerational Effects and Concern for Future Generations

[A] conclusion that emerged from the five most recent studies was that the probability of harm for exposure to persistent toxic chemicals, including organochlorines, is greater for the progeny of exposed individuals than for the exposed individuals themselves. (Jack Vallentyne, for the Athabasca Tribal Council, Edmonton: 4919)

Wayland Swain, one of the experts on toxicology for the Government of the Northwest Territories, presented evidence on the presence of PCB (a molecule related to dioxin whose equivalent toxicity is 40 per cent that of dioxin)[12] in the systems of families of Great Lakes fishermen who ate fish meals 1-3.5 times a week. Swain's review of studies of the families, especially the pregnant mothers and newborn children, showed that "we are dealing with a unique set of toxicants . . . affecting not the individual exposed, but the progeny that the individual bears." He found evidence in the scientific literature of "transplacental transmission of organic contaminants" and health effects such as reduced birth weight, smaller head size, reduced gestational age, immature autonomic motor systems, a four-point drop in IQ per generation, and poorer fine motor skills. Swain concluded, "what I can tell you is that very critical human tissues are becoming affected by toxic substances."[13]

Swain's evidence of the intergenerational impact of toxins linked the issue of health risks for fish eaters to the slow, invisible genocide of native people. Cindy Gilday argued:

[T]here was a medical doctor from Calgary that said if we wanted to commit genocide, as far as Native people are concerned, releasing the chlorinated organics is a sure way to do it. . . . I feel like I am listening all over again to the smallpox blanket scenario, but this time it is six generations. (Edmonton: 5927-5928)[14]

Swain's conclusions were of great concern to Review Board members, as is shown by the fact that they quoted his presentation at length in their report as a justification for the recommendation to postpone construction of the mill until studies had been done to show that the mill effluent would not produce harmful downstream effects.[15]

Many people who testified in hearing locations downstream from the proposed Alpac mill expressed concern that they were the recipients of pollution that they did not create, and no government agency seemed willing or able to help them:

> I've tried to think of words to describe what has happened here: Unfair, unjust, lunacy, even criminal; but none of them seems to capture the simple truth. What word describes when people are deliberately destroying others and themselves for the immediate gain, while people who are being destroyed watch without fighting back, and the people who are supposed to protect us all make excuses to allow the whole thing to continue. (Gerry Cheezie, Dene Nation, Fort Resolution: 3697)

To many of those who spoke at the hearings, it seemed reasonable to believe that intergenerational effects should be fundamental to health and environmental policy. This native woman communicated a perspective shared by many native Canadians:

> We are so blind and uneducated by this colonized society, that the majority of aboriginal peoples cannot see anything that is not immediate except this colonization. We have forgotten the aboriginal philosophy which states that when making any major decisions, we should look ahead at least seven generations, meaning our children, our children's children, our grandchildren's children and so on. I beg of you please look to the future and stop this destruction now. Please do not continue to persist in this multinational destruction. Do not ignore the history. Observe native rights and substantial philosophies. (Geraldine Manossa, Athabasca: 3127)

Fish Consumption: Local Knowledge or Expert Knowledge?

The story of ethnocentrism was complicated and somewhat confused by the conclusions about fish consumption drawn in a second review of the proposed mill (the Jaakko Pöyry Report, discussed in Chapter 8). One such conclusion was that "inhabitants of the Lake Athabasca area and the Wood Buffalo Park consume less fish than was initially estimated."[16] More specifically:

[T]he native peoples of the Lake Athabasca area (Fort Chipewyan) and of the Wood Buffalo National Park area (Fort Smith) have present day fish consumption patterns which are significantly lower than the average Canadian's (roughly one quarter) and that as a result they are very unlikely to be at risk of exceeding allowable intakes of chemicals such as dioxin as a result of fish consumption, irrespective of whether or not the Alpac project is allowed to proceed. (Jaakko Pöyry Report: 123)

This conclusion, which ran counter to that of the Alpac EIA Review Board, was based on information from a recent Ph.D. thesis by Eleanor Wein.[17] Wein studied the frequency, amount, and seasonal variation in the use of country foods, including large and small mammals, fish, and berries, in the native communities of Fort Smith, on the Slave River, and Fort Chipewyan, on Lake Athabasca.

A series of letters from David Schindler, a member of the Alpac EIA Review Board, and Wein herself, made it clear that Jaakko Pöyry had misquoted Wein's thesis, calculated fish consumption incorrectly, and made other mistakes. For example, the Jaakko Pöyry Report stated that the "average Canadian" eats 98 grams of fish per week, quoting Wein's thesis. However, nowhere in Wein's thesis, or in any of her subsequent publications, did she mention a figure for fish consumption of the "average Canadian." In fact, the figure of 98 grams of fish per week represented the average intake across her native study sample. This simple error falsified all of Jaakko Pöyry's further calculations and conclusions about the health risk to natives from eating fish from the Slave River and Lake Athabasca.[18] This mistake is especially noteworthy given that the authors of the Jaakko Pöyry Report explicitly chose to discount anecdotal evidence about fish consumption given by many native people at the hearings in favour of "expert" evidence, (that is, their interpretation of Wein's data) even though they recognized a large discrepancy between the two forms of evidence.[19] In so doing, these authors demonstrated their bias against local knowledge and in favour of expert testimony.

The problem with the Canadian health standard for acceptable levels of dioxin in fish cannot be corrected simply with more careful measurements and calculations. The problem was created by the assumptions that all Canadians eat the same amount of fish as the average person from Central Canada, and that no one eats fish liver. Correcting the problem requires overcoming ignorance and unwitting ethnocentric bias. Holding public hearings in locations downstream from the pulp mill allowed participants from these locations to contribute their knowledge of local conditions and practices, and the role these practices play in traditional native ways of life, and to help correct the faulty assumptions. In Chapter 6, we examine in more detail the question of how local knowledge can complement and correct expert testimony.

Notes

1. We would like to thank Bill Fuller who co-authored an earlier version of this chapter in the paper "Ethnocentrism in Scientific Standards," reproduced in *Stability and Change in Nature: Ecological and Cultural Dimensions* (International Forum for Biophilosophy, Conference Preprints, Budapest, Hungary, March 1992).

2. This and all further citations of the Alpac EIA Main Report in this chapter refer to Alberta-Pacific Forest Industries Inc., *Alberta Pacific Forest Industries Inc. Environmental Impact Assessment: Bleached Kraft Pulp Mill Main Report* (Edmonton, Alberta: Alberta-Pacific Forest Industries Inc., 1989). This citation cites R. H. Voss, "Trace organic contaminants in pulp and paper mill effluents and their environmental effects" (*Pulp and Paper Research Institute of Canada, Miscellaneous Reports* No. 112).

3. All items identified as "Filed Documents" are written submissions to the Alpac EIA Review Board, a collection of the Filed Documents is housed in the Athabasca University Library; quotations from the Alberta-Pacific EIA Review Board public hearings are from J. G. Moore and Associates Ltd., *The Alberta-Pacific Environment Impact Assessment Review Board Public Hearing Proceedings, Volumes 1-55* (Edmonton, Alberta: J. G. Moore and Associates Ltd., 1989).

4. Alberta-Pacific Forest Industries Inc., *Alberta-Pacific Forest Industries Inc., Written Submissions and Responses Volumes 1, 2 and 3* (Edmonton, Alberta: Alberta-Pacific Forest Industries Inc., 1989): Responses to Mr. and Mrs. Kostyk, Response 12, p. 236.

5. This and all further citations of the Review Board Report in this chapter refer to Alberta-Pacific Environmental Impact Assessment Review Board, *The Proposed Alberta-Pacific Pulp Mill: Report of the EIA Review Board*, March 1990 (Edmonton, Alberta: Alberta Environment, 1990).

6. Review Board Report, p. 22. 2,3,7,8-TCDF is considered one-tenth as toxic as 2,3,7,8-TCDD, although its concentrations are usually ten-fold higher in pulp-mill effluent.

7. See, for example, Bob Willes, Edmonton: 5978-6008.

8. Health standards for dioxin concentrations in fish differ in different juris-dictions. For example, the US standard is much more stringent than

Canada's, because American authorities are not convinced that there is a dioxin threshold. Recent reports suggest that evidence downplaying the links between human health problems and exposure to agent orange, dioxin, or both, was falsified. See Appellate Court of Illinois, 5th District. No 5-88-0420, 3 October 1989; F. Rohleder, "Cause of Death in Workers Exposed to Dioxins at BASF, Ludwigshafen, Germany, in 1953," (Paper delivered at the 9th International Symposium of Chlorinated Dioxins and Related Compounds, Toronto, Ontario, 17-22 September, 1989).

9. Chief Bonnet Rouge, Fort Resolution: 3546.

10. Schindler has noted that, "When Dr. Wein's data are used as a basis, it is obvious that current Health and Welfare Guidelines of 20 parts per trillion as dioxin equivalents would allow native people to consume amounts in excess of this value. Indeed, in the vicinity of bleached kraft mills already on the Peace and Athabasca rivers, persons consuming as much fish as these aboriginal populations would be consuming several times the maximum desirable levels." In "A Critique of Proposed Federal Regulations for Pulp and Paper Effluent and Recent Evidence Implicating Dioxins as Hazards to Human Health," unpublished, 1991, p. 8.

11. Letter from E. E. Wein to D. Schindler, in Submission #5 to Alberta-Pacific Scientific Review Panel, "Possible Effects of the Proposed Alberta Pacific Mill on the Athabasca River—Comments on Proposed Mitigation Measures," by D. Schindler, August 21, 1990, p. 3.

12. PCB was used as an index: it actually included all other toxic substances present in Lake Michigan fish, including chlorinated organics (Swain, Edmonton: 5874).

13. Swain, Edmonton: 5871-5880.

14. Blankets that had been exposed to smallpox were used by colonial powers in various locations in Canada, the US, and elsewhere to exterminate native people. Smallpox was devastating to native communities as the populations had no previous exposure to the disease, and no natural defences against it.

15. Review Board Report, pp. 22-24, 32.

16. This and all further citations of the Jaakko Pöyry Report in this chapter refer to Jaakko Pöyry, *Complementary Scientific Review of the Proposed Alberta-Pacific Pulp Mill Project Environmental Impact Assessment* (Helsinki, Finland: Jaakko Pöyry, Oy, 1990). This citation quotes the Executive Summary, p. e6.

17. E. E. Wein, "Nutrient Intakes and Use of Country Foods by Native Canadians near Wood Buffalo National Park" (Ph.D. Diss., University of Guelph, 1989).

18. D. Schindler, letter to Hon. Ralph Klein, Minister of Environment, July 30, 1990, p. 1. This letter, the Schindler-Wein correspondence and Jaakko Pöyry's response are in Submission #5 to the Alberta-Pacific Scientific Review Panel, "Possible Effects of the Proposed Alberta-Pacific Mill on the Athabasca River—Comments on Proposed Mitigation Measures," by David Schindler, August 21, 1990 .

19. Jaakko Pöyry Report, p. 118.

"[O]ur research indicates that the impact of the pulp mill on agriculture will
be minimal . . . ."
(Alpac, Written Submissions and Responses: 47)
(Photograph courtesy of *The Athabasca Advocate*)

CHAPTER 6

Questions of Authority: Experts, Counter-experts, and Local Knowledge

We also wish to commend . . . the Department of Environment for their input in making this the most environmentally safe kraft mill. Let's have faith in the experts of environmental concern. Alberta Provincial Government is a forerunner in this field, with expertise in many areas of environment. Let them do their job. (Walter Harrynuck, Mayor of Boyle, Prosperity: 7457-7458)[1]

Alberta-Pacific is the party or participant in these proceedings who has brought the most coherent set of experts . . . on virtually every issue that has been raised in the course of the Environmental Impact Assessment, including this hearing, and . . . when you look at the whole of the evidence . . . and, in particular, the focused expert evidence which has been produced in these proceedings and . . . in the technical submissions . . . that is the material you should rely on. (Dennis Thomas, lawyer for Alberta-Pacific, Prosperity: 7587-7588)

I have learned that people that have the name "Doctor" in front of their names don't always know everything. I used to be intimidated by people like that, but that will be no longer. (Ron Epp, Review Board member, Prosperity: 7633)

In Chapter 5 we heard people from the Northwest Territories presenting their concerns about eating fish contaminated with dioxins, furans, and other chlorinated organic compounds. In presenting their case, these people drew on their knowledge of traditional native culture. In this chapter, we tell a different story of public participation in the EIA hearings. We move closer to the immediate impact area of the mill, and listen to people who presented concerns based, not on native cultures or traditions, but on other sources of detailed knowledge of the local area. It shows how some of the presentations made by expert witnesses on behalf of the company and the Alberta government were challenged by people in the communities around the proposed mill site, and how people with knowledge of the area provided information on concerns not addressed by the experts.

Various opinions were expressed by public participants on the quality of the expert evidence in the technical documents supporting the project. At one end of the spectrum were those, including the Mayor of Boyle who is cited in the opening quotation to this chapter, who recommended full, unquestioning acceptance. At the other end were those who criticized the apparent willingness of the proponent to draw conclusions on the basis of inadequate evidence:

> [The EIA goes on to say that] "There is a large uncertainty in the emission rate estimates for the cooling pond." And that, "The rates are educated guesses." . . . I am a household engineer. And in my educated opinion, and I am educated, two degrees, this is bullshit science. Where do you get off making enigmatic predictions that will effect my lungs and those of my family? (Merilyn Peruniak, Athabasca: 3330-3331)

What is an expert, and what is the expert's role in environmental public hearings? A presenter from Fort Smith offered this definition:

> What I would consider an expert is [a] pretty legalistic type of definition of an expert. Someone who is trained in a specific area and is highly regarded by his peers. And who can be relied on to give unbiased and accurate technical advice on an issue . . . a real good expert is going to tell his client the way he sees it, rather than the way he thinks his client wants him to portray it. The client then filters what he

wants to hear and presents his side of the story. I still think a client can have good experts working for him, or a proponent can have good experts and can present good evidence. That does not mean that they do, but they can. (Jack Van Camp)[2]

In a paper on the politics of technology,[3] Michael McDonald describes experts as "insiders" who are "usually lined up on the side of the more powerful institutions in our society—corporations and bureaucracies." Experts typically think of themselves as professionals in such areas as cost-benefit analysis, toxicology, or industrial design, having claims to authority and power on the basis of their possession of bodies of knowledge not accessible to "outsiders." Along with the presumption of authority comes a belief in professional hegemony, "the belief that in the area of technical expertise, which is defined by the profession, issues are to be decided by rigorous standards of evidence and argument, which again the profession defines." The Mayor of Boyle's confidence in experts is an example of acceptance of the authority of scientists and specialists.[4] The authority and legitimacy of expert knowledge and the tools used by experts, such as the LC50 test discussed in Chapter 4, are seldom questioned. Even counter-experts—experts hired, often by environmental groups, to challenge the data and conclusions drawn by company or government experts—seldom question the authority of their discipline and its tools.

At the Alpac hearings, members of the public were made aware that their presentations were in a different category from those of the experts, and that their testimony was not considered to contain technical information:

> [T]here is a significant amount of technical information which the Board has yet to receive . . . It's imperative that we have such information. We want to hear from the public, but we must have that technical information as well. (Gerry DeSorcy, Review Board chairman, Athabasca: 3291)

The Review Board chairman's remarks made clear to public participants that their knowledge would carry less weight than that of experts. In spite of this imbalance, however, many people came forward to report on their knowledge of local conditions and their assessment of how a pulp mill would affect their lives and livelihoods. In this chapter we present four examples of the mill's anticipated impact on the community—the removal of agricultural land from production, atmospheric emissions, increased traffic, and economic benefits—and show how local people challenged the authority of experts. In doing so, they revealed that the company and the government downplayed, or failed to take into account, several critical changes that could take place in their community.

Taking Agricultural Land Out of Production: A Question of Acres and Productivity

[O]ur research indicates that the impact of the pulp mill on agriculture will be minimal. Some land will be permanently taken out of production and Alberta Pacific recognizes this as an impact. (Alpac, Written Responses: 47)[5]

The site selected for the Alpac pulp mill was located in the middle of an established farming community known as Prosperity. The farms in the Prosperity area are productive by local standards, and the sense of community is strong. A pulp mill had never been built in an agricultural region in Alberta before, but the government and the company assured residents that the impacts on their lives would be minimal. Many farmers rejected this claim, and cross-examined company and government officials about the loss of agricultural land to industrial use, and about the productivity of their soil.

Loss of agricultural land is considered to be a significant land-use issue by the federal government, because only eleven per cent of Canada's total land area is capable of agricultural production, and less than five per cent is capable of producing a wide range of crops.[6] Alpac used the Canada Land Inventory (CLI) system of rating soil capability to back its claim that the agricultural land taken out of production for the pulp mill contained low-quality soil. [The CLI classifies soils with severe limitations to agriculture as Class 4, and soils with moderately severe limitations as Class 3.]

[Two hundred and twenty-seven hectares] will be lost to agricultural production for the duration of the project as they will be occupied by facilities. These lands are rated under the Canada Land Inventory system as having a Class 4 capability for agriculture . . . with the exception of sixteen hectares along the route of the effluent pipeline, which has a Class 3 capability. (Alpac EIA Main Report: Appendix 3, p. 3-4.4)[7]

Alpac's use of CLI classifications to emphasize the poor quality of the soil taken out of agricultural production appeared to legitimate the decision to locate the mill in this farming community. But the company neglected to mention that almost all the farm land in Athabasca county is of Classes 3 and 4, and that although it is limited in capability, it is well suited to certain crops and to livestock farming. Furthermore, although the CLI classification of soils may be accurate, it is farming methods that determine soil productivity. Several farmers challenged the company's interpretation of the CLI classifications of their land by offering their own accounts of its productivity:

> We find it also very disturbing that the EIA and supplemental documentation released by Alpac keep referring to this area as Class 4 soil with limited agricultural production capabilities. I wish to bring to the attention of the panel our production averages for the past three years on our major crops and compare them to the regional averages based on data obtained from the Alberta Hail and Crop Insurance records. Our production average for wheat, 50 bushels per acre; Alberta Hail and Crop average 30 bushels per acre. Our production average for barley, 75 bushels per acre; Alberta Hail and Crop average 45 bushels per acre. Our production average for canola, 25 bushels per acre; Alberta Hail and Crop average 17 bushels per acre. Do these figures sound like the soil has limited capabilities? (Eli and Nellie Cholach, Prosperity: 7327)

Another farmer echoed this testimony:

> I am a local cow/calf producer . . . My home is about three and a half miles southeast of the proposed pulp mill. . . . I would like to start with agricultural uniqueness in the area. . . . For proof of this . . . in the year 1988 when most of Alberta had a poor crop . . . we had a bumper crop in this area. In 1984, most of southern Alberta had a total forage crop failure; again, we had a good forage crop. In the year

1984, southern cattle producers were able to save their basic herds by buying hay from farmers in this area. Why is it important to save the basic herd? Because it takes ten years to establish a good working herd. In this way, we serve as a buffer for other parts of the province. When their crops fail, we usually still get a crop and sometimes a bumper crop. This has been true from the time this area was settled. (Dennis Rybicki, Grassland: 6855)

The provincial government and Alpac also addressed the amount of agricultural land needed for the pulp-mill site, but it wasn't until farmers pressed for clarification that everyone realized just how many acres would be lost. There was not only land for the mill site, but also land for bridges, rail lines, roads, and rights-of-way. Only after probing by a local farmer was the true extent of land lost to agriculture revealed:

Emil Zachkewich: I wonder if you could comment on . . . the road impacts? . . . What amount of agricultural land will each one of these three alternatives [for proposed roads] be taking out of production?

Jack Phelps (Alberta Transportation representative): . . . with respect to agricultural lands, the total acreages required for Alternative 1 from Class 3 lands . . . would be 14.6 acres; Class 4 lands would be 16.5 acres. For Alternative 2, from Class 3 would be 8.5 acres; from Class 4 would be 13 acres. For Alternative 3, from Class 3 would be 20 acres; from Class 4 would be 22.9 acres. (Prosperity: 3752-3753)

Between 21 and 43 acres didn't seem like much additional land to lose for a road to service this mega-project. But farmers knew their land like the backs of their hands. They understood space, distance, and acres from calculating seeding rates in the spring, from putting in fence posts in the summer, and from sitting on a tractor, whether tilling, ploughing, or feeding livestock, the rest of the year. Farmers knew the acreage taken up by gullies, wet areas, patches of trees, and road allowances. It was with this intimate understanding of space, not from a map in a civil servant's office, and not from a quick look from the cab of a company truck travelling at highway speeds through the countryside, that a Review

Board member, who was also a farmer, challenged the figures cited by Phelps:

> Mike Franchuk: I was never that good at math and I was just wondering, could you please add the amount of acres taken out of production as far as agriculture is concerned?

> Phelps: The numbers I gave were total kilometres of length, not acres. I am not sure of the total number of agricultural acres that will be removed. The total acreage required for additional right-of-way over what exists is 287 acres for Alternative 1; 293 for Alternative 2; and 207 for Alternative 3. (Prosperity: 3760)

Franchuk's question forced a recognition that the government had erred in reporting length (kilometres) instead of area (hectares or acres). For example, Alternative 1 would require 287 acres, rather than the total of 31 acres given by Phelps. Not only had the government experts underestimated by five to ten times the actual acreage to be taken out of production, but they had also lacked sufficient experience on the land to realize that something was wrong with their calculations.

Consequences of Atmospheric Emissions for Farming and for Health

> [M]ill atmospheric emissions will be below the concentrations that affect either humans or livestock, and no project related health issues have been identified. (Alpac EIA Main Report: 4.35)

> My family and I live and farm eight miles southeast from the proposed pulp mill site. Most of our land is north of our home place, and is much closer to the site. . . . Let me tell you, there was an awful lot of sweat and tears shed to develop what we have today. It just didn't happen overnight. Most of the land we farm is not marginal, but perhaps close to some of the best in Alberta. On the farm today we grow a garden, we grow fruits for home canning, and pick wild berries of all types for our own use. We also grow wheat, canola, barley, and raise beef cattle for market. The air we

breathe feels fresh and clean. There is no smell that we can
identify . . . . To put it briefly, we like it here and want to
remain living here, but now we have a great concern. In fact,
at times we are a bit scared and get good and angry.
(Walter Aleksiuk, Prosperity: 7458-7459)

Even more contentious than the loss of agricultural land to
industry was the issue of air quality. The Review Board reported that
"The principal concerns of local citizens and others respecting
emissions to the atmosphere relate to sulphur and chlorine
compounds, oxides of nitrogen, water emissions and particulates
which might cause fog, and odours."[8]

Alpac estimated that fifteen tonnes of sulphur dioxide would be
emitted into the air each day.[9] Many people worried that these
emissions could affect land and water, livestock, apiaries, produce,
and human health. One concern brought out in the hearings was
that not enough research had been done on the effects of sulphur
deposition on livestock. A cattle producer outlined her frustration
with the lack of research on sulphur emissions this way:

This is cattle country. Driving along the road you can see
cows just about on every field. Now, what effect will this mill
have on animals? I asked questions; tried to find some
information. Nothing. I thought perhaps some science
magazine could write something up, some books. No,
nothing.

At last, here it was, the Alberta Environmental Supplement.
Here is how much they said about it. Sulphur emissions may
cause higher levels of sulphur in ruminant fed animals,
resulting in selenium deficiencies in cattle. This deficiency
may lead to white muscle disease in animals . . . [W]e
already supplement our cattle with salt on our farm. And
yet, some of the calves show signs of white muscle disease.
. . . Do we already have more sulphur in the air than these
animals can tolerate? (Mary Rybicki, Grassland: 6858-6860)

Rybicki's son questioned how decisions could be made with
insufficient data, and asked for protection:

In my opinion, a superficial soil study and an animal health study that begins by stating "there have been few studies concerning the effects of SO_2 on wildlife and farm animals" . . . is totally inadequate.

I would like to take this opportunity to ask for a baseline study on all aspects of agriculture in this area and long-term monitoring so that we, the farmers of the area, will be able to prove damage, if it has or has not occurred.
(Dennis Rybicki, Grassland: 6856)

As local people came forward, they painted a complex picture of farming in the community. The concerns they raised were as varied as local farming practices. For example, farmers use dugouts (excavations that collect rain and melting snow) to store water for their stock and households. This speaker brought to the Review Board's attention his concern about an aspect of water quality that was not addressed in the EIA:

On our farmstead close by we have two dugouts. The one to the east of the yard shows up from the spring run-off, but in a short period, the water disappears into the ground. The dugout to the west of the yard . . . was dug . . . 12 feet deep into the water table . . . After the spring run-off, it fills up, but the water level drops down a certain amount. That means that the water is forced into the water table. As the snow melts in the spring, it will bring in the deposits from the pulp mill emissions, entering into our dugouts and also entering the water table. I wonder how many dugouts there may be in the community of this nature? (Nick Zilinski, Prosperity: 7481-7482)

There are rows of bee hives at the edge of many farmers' fields in Athabasca county. Alberta clover honey enjoys a world market, but air pollution could affect both quality and sales:

[The honey industry] is closely regulated and monitored as to levels of contamination in the product. For example, the present level of phenol allowable is two parts per million. Our local background level is one part per million. We have very little capacity to absorb any increase in that area. . . . The honeybee gathers water from any available source and uses it for hive cooling. The end result is that the residues become concentrated and incorporated into the food product . . . what effect will the proposed mill have on our industry? Specifically, how will it affect phenol levels, hydrogen sulphide levels, and other organic chlorine compounds? Our product is seen as one of the finest in the world, and one of the cleanest, and that ensures our market.

If you don't work in the areas that deal with contaminations in parts per million, you don't really have any insight into what it looks like . . . last year I produced one semi-load of honey, seventy 45-gallon drums. Contamination of two parts per million would equal one 45-gram chocolate bar dissolved in that load. So we are talking about very small quantities. (Arno Birkigt, beekeeper, Athabasca: 3077-3079)

Alpac replied to Birkigt's concern about contamination of his honey by sending him a letter pointing out that a beekeeper had produced award-winning honey near the pulp mill of Alpac's parent company. Mr. Birkigt was not persuaded, and at a subsequent hearing apprised the Review Board of a misleading aspect of the response:

The second part of the response dealt with Sheep Creek Apiaries from Skookumchuk, BC, suggesting that since they won first prize at the Royal Agricultural Winter Fair 56th show, that all would be well. . . . This is misleading because the honey was judged only on colour. There was no testing for contamination. (Arno Birkigt, Prosperity: 6732-6733)

Organic farmers were also troubled, because pollution from the mill would affect the quality of their produce and its certification as well:

I just wanted to really affirm that we are organic farmers, and you did hear the report on the bee industry, and it will affect us the same. All that we sell is going to be seriously tested and it's really going to affect the way we live. (Pat Bellamy, Prosperity: 3940)

People who worried about atmospheric emissions from the mill pointed out that Alpac had rejected one site for the mill partly because of "its close proximity to the Town of Athabasca from the point of view of . . . air (odour, inversions, etc.)."[10] Yet there are a number of communities near the site selected for the mill. As area resident Nick Zilinski put it, "This sets a double standard."[11]

Alpac replied:

> [Y]our comment about a double standard with respect to air emissions is understandable. When the site selection study was completed, there was as yet no air emission data available, and so some very conservative (i.e. worst case) assumptions were made. It is now known that the air emissions will be very much better than was assumed at the time, and the air quality considerations set out in the site selection study are therefore no longer relevant. (Alpac, Written Responses: 91)

It was frustrating for people who were trying to check the claims made by the company to be told in the middle of the hearing that information in the EIA should be disregarded, and that new data from unnamed sources should be accepted. Not everyone was impressed with the new data on sulphur dioxide. A consultant hired by a local farmer told the Review Board that "reducing the sulphur dioxide emissions by a factor of six at the drop of a hat is a neat trick," and wondered whether Alpac had also "conveniently lowered" estimates on nitrogen oxide emissions.[12]

In the months prior to the hearings, many people had raised concerns about health impacts from atmospheric emissions, yet the Alpac EIA contained only one short paragraph on the subject, which concluded that local concerns were unsubstantiated (see the opening quotation for this section). In the one and one-half page appendix covering both aquatic and atmospheric emissions of the mill, Alpac's consulting toxicologist, J. D. Taylor, concluded that mill atmospheric emissions would be below the concentrations that would affect either humans or livestock.[13] His conclusion was based on a total of six references, including one personal communication, none of which referred to chlorinated organic compounds. Such sparse analysis was an affront to local people who felt their concerns were being belittled. A local farmer drew the Board's attention to a recent study from a pulp-mill town.

According to Dr. Robert Dykes from the North Hawke Medical Clinic, Prince George with its kraft mill has a mortality rate 34 per cent higher and a cancer rate 46 per cent higher than the rest of the province. If the pulp mill goes into operations and the death rate and the cancer rate rises here like it has in Prince George, some of us will pay a very, very high price. (Ted Pitman, Prosperity: 7169)

As there had been no industrial development in the Athabasca region, many people asked for baseline health studies so that future health patterns could be contrasted with present trends in cancer or respiratory diseases in humans, and so that impacts on animal health, such as livestock abortion and infertility, could be monitored. The public remembered that in the ranching country of southern Alberta, no baseline health studies were conducted before construction of the huge Waterton gas plants, and that it had not been proved whether or not there were effects on human and animal health from sulphur and other gas well emissions.

When I attended public meetings prior to the release of the EIA, people living close to mega-projects said over and over, don't let them in until there is a baseline health study. They say we can't prove our health problems are caused by the project. (Mary Richardson, Athabasca: 3460)

Ellie Robson, a consultant who prepared a presentation on the impact of pulp mills on health, argued that conventional toxicology and epidemiology were designed to investigate the health effects of single toxins, not the synergistic effects of the hundreds of chemicals encountered in everyday life.

Neither [toxicology nor epidemiology] were intended to answer the questions posed in environmental impact assessment . . . it appears that the linear cause/effect approach is inadequate for environmental health research. Research methods that can accommodate multiple cause and effect scenarios over extensive time frames need to be developed. (Ellie Robson, Filed Document G-62: 3)

Although members of the public concerned about effects of atmospheric emissions from the mill on soils and animal and human health made several interventions, the Review Board agreed with the proponent that the public had little to worry about. The Board did, however, recommend monitoring of various sorts:

> The Review Board finds the proposed mill acceptable in terms of effects of emissions to the atmosphere. However, appropriate monitoring of air and soil is needed, including the gathering of base-line data prior to operations. If the mill is to be located in a developed community, very special effort is needed to minimize odour-causing releases, and to investigate odour complaints. (Review Board Report: 57)

> Because the Review Board does not see the proposed mill as a significant threat to local residents, it does not believe a health study of the area, as requested by some, is warranted. (Review Board Report: 67)

More Traffic of a Different Kind

The transportation infrastructure required by the Alpac mill would be extensive. Logging roads would be built throughout wilderness areas. Logging trucks would also be using the local highways and rural roads to deliver trees logged on private land. The mill would receive chemicals and industrial supplies, and ship its product to market, by both road and rail. Workers would commute to the pulp mill every day, from several directions. All of this activity would require well-built roads, rail lines, and bridges, often far from the mill site itself.

Alpac discussed the socio-economic impacts of truck traffic in one paragraph of its EIA:

> Truck traffic into the mill will largely consist of trucks supplying either logs or chips. The majority of truck traffic will originate in the Calling Lake-Wabasca area and will use the new proposed highway connecting to the mill site via a new bridge across the Athabasca River. Another major truck traffic flow will come from the northeast via Highway 63, the

remainder of the traffic being shared between Highway 55 east and west. Gross vehicle weights of 60 tonnes will be used in the transport of logs to the site. A network of off-highway logging roads will eventually be built to minimize the amount of logging traffic on provincial highways. (Alpac EIA Main Report: 5.12-5.13)

The Government of Alberta requested that Alpac address the impacts of pulp-mill traffic on existing traffic loads and the effects of increased traffic on tourism. Alpac responded that "the increase in traffic" would be "about 25 per cent," and "the impact upon summer tourists is expected to be minimal."[14] People in the local community reminded the Review Board, the government, and Alpac that an assessment of the impacts of increased truck traffic involved not simply a description of the routes the traffic would be using or a figure indicating increased traffic loads. Neither the EIA nor the supplemental information tabled by Alpac adequately addressed the question of how mill traffic would affect traditional uses of roads, accident rates, school bus routes, road maintenance, and driving conditions—all issues that concerned people in the local communities.

An important aspect of local people's concerns was the way disparate factors could work together as ingredients in a recipe for disaster. This is the kind of phenomenon that traditional environmental impact assessment is ill-equipped to handle, as an EIA typically looks at factors one at a time. For example, as was pointed out, it is not enough to consider simply how many school bus routes will share roads with logging trucks—what if these roads are often foggy? This neglect of the complexity of transportation issues raised many questions from the public. Highway 620 Advocates, a citizens' group that lobbied for improved road safety in another area of Alberta, submitted a letter outlining "the adverse effect of the traffic change that occurs when the proposed mill uses public highways to supply its wood. This traffic adjustment not only damages the road, it compromises public safety for the sake of the logging industry."[15] The local woman who contacted Highway 620 Advocates pursued some of their concerns at the hearing:

I asked [Highway 620 Advocates] if they had had any trouble with school buses, and they said that there have been five near misses. In one instance, a school bus was stopped on the highway, and a logging truck coming up behind could not stop in time. The logging truck passed the school bus on the right-hand side, it went down into the ditch, and around and up onto the other side . . . the truck tire marks are still there. (Merilyn Peruniak, Prosperity: 7557)

Industrial use of the roadways in an agricultural region raised new concerns about road safety; logging trucks and transport trucks carrying hazardous chemicals would compete for road space with school buses and slow-moving farm machinery, children riding bicycles, families visiting, shopping or getting their mail, and game animals or loose livestock. Also, maps don't indicate areas known to locals where fog collects, where traffic congests, where there are icy patches or where roads get rutted quickly after a rain because they were not built for industrial traffic.

What about incompatibility of slow-moving farm vehicles with logging and chemical trucks on the highways at peak farming times? Will farm vehicle insurance rates go up? Will car insurance rates go up in general? (Merilyn Peruniak, Athabasca: 3328)

As a result of these questions and others, Alberta Transportation was asked to provide comparative statistics of truck and traffic accidents for a logging and sawmill district in northern Alberta.[16] However, the area studied had neither the number of farms nor the volume of agricultural traffic that Prosperity did; nor was its population similar to that of Prosperity. Furthermore, the RCMP data did not specify which accidents involved logging trucks.

Confusion arose over just how many logging trucks would be on the roads, because Alpac specified only the number of loaded trucks entering the mill site, not the total number of trucks going both ways. Some people found the manner in which Alpac presented truck volumes misleading:

We have to share the road to Athabasca, the centre we use most, with these same logging trucks, the supply trucks and the commuters to the mill. And please remember that logging trucks don't just go into the mill, they come out, too, empty. The daily average of truckloads of wood supplied to the mill in the winter is given [in the EIA] as 481. So you can double that, for a total of 962 trips per day in the winter converging, on, or emerging from the mill. . . . And this, in the winter, when road conditions are at their worst. The potential for disaster is great. No matter how you look at it, there is no positive aspect of this mill that will make up for one person's death. (Merilyn Peruniak, Athabasca: 3326-3327)

Mike Gismondi: I have always found it very confusing. You say 400 trucks a day are going by your house, but really, it means 800 trucks a day are going to go by your house, doesn't it? It means 400 times when they come in full, and then do they go back the same way?

Jack Phelps (Alberta Transportation representative): Yes, the numbers I gave you were, I think, were 230 on the Calling Lake road, so that would be 460; and 175 on the Highway 63 one, so that would be 350. (Prosperity: 3755)

In bringing up the many issues about increased traffic that had not been considered by the government or by Alpac, local people were their own best experts, with a wealth of experience and observation. Local knowledge of road conditions and an informed understanding of existing local traffic patterns was invaluable for assessing environmental impacts. Not only safety, but also the effect of building access roads through farms, wetlands or wildlife habitat were of concern. Especially important was the fact that local people thought of these factors not only individually, but in terms of how they might work together to present a threat to public safety and the viability of farming in the area.

Local Economic Benefits

Annual municipal taxes payable by Alberta-Pacific to the County of Athabasca could range from $1.6 million to $4 million. (Alpac EIA Main Report: 5.11)

And I have to say that as far as women are concerned, I don't really feel that this company actually gives a damn whether women have jobs in this project or not. (Rita Egan, Edmonton: 5041)

The promise of a massive infusion of capital and hundreds of jobs raised expectations that the pulp mill would solve the problems of unemployment in the Athabasca area and provide great economic benefits. Unemployment rates in Athabasca county ranged from ten to seventeen per cent, substantially higher than the provincial urban rate of from nine to eleven per cent in 1989-1990. In surrounding native communities unemployment rates ranged from 50 to 70 per cent. Alpac projected that 50 per cent of the construction jobs and half of the 440 permanent mill jobs would go to local people. Moreover, the company would pay millions of dollars every year in property taxes. Some local people, however, wondered who would benefit and whether the benefits would be as great as predicted. For example, it was women who pointed out that the discussion of numbers of jobs failed to acknowledge that what was really being talked about was jobs for men.

As a woman, I cannot help noticing that the Alpac panel of experts and management is all male. The only women would seem to occupy clerical positions. Now, I don't say this with any suggestion of discrimination, as I would assume there are very few women who have the necessary training for these jobs, I am just saying that I see very little evidence of good job opportunities for women here. I would like to see specific information on job opportunities.

According to Statistics Canada's information for 1986, females made up 43.28 per cent of the Alberta labour force. Bear in mind that many of these women are single parents who are the sole breadwinners for their families . . . goods-producing industries, such as the proposed pulp mill, employ only 14.11 per cent, while service industries employ 85.89 per cent. Perhaps we should be concentrating on a different area of job creation, so that we are not almost excluding nearly half of our work force. (Ann Stiles Athabasca: 3300-3301)

No mention is made of women [in the EIA]. Women make up nearly half, 44 per cent, of the labour force in the Athabasca area, yet no mention is made of women in the company's hiring practices. Does the mill plan any affirmative action to ensure a specified number of women

are hired for higher-paying non-traditional mill jobs? Are any initiatives such as training programs, child care provisions, et cetera, being planned to help women overcome obstacles they traditionally face?
(Diana Salomaa, Athabasca: 2898)

Questions were also raised about how much the company would pay in property taxes. The tax issue needed clarification because the estimates made by county officials were significantly higher than those stated by Alpac in its EIA.

Joan Sherman: Could you explain to me the actual taxes that you expect to get annually from Alpac? . . . at the Development Appeal Board hearing, Alpac said somewhere between $1.6 and $4 million, and you just said $4 million. Could you please elaborate on that?

R. A. Wilkinson (Reeve, County of Athabasca): I think the figures that were in the original environmental impact assessment study stated by Alpac were a minimum of $4 million.

Sherman: A minimum of $4 million?

Jim Woodward (County Administrator): The figure of $4 million . . . was determined after consultation with the assessors that work from the Municipal Assessment Branch. . . . We believe that $4 million figure is most likely . . . conservative. In fact, when the mill is fully operational, the taxes would be substantially higher. (Athabasca: 2568-2570)

When asked to comment, Alpac's Gerry Fenner replied:

I can't comment on the specifics of that because that's an assessment process. What we did was put into the document what we felt would be the range.

Mike Gismondi: I'm puzzled . . . that we can measure dioxins in parts per quadrillion, but we can't measure taxes except in a range from $1.6 to $4 million. (Athabasca: 2577)

Despite the promise of an increased tax base, some residents feared a dramatic increase in local taxation to pay for the municipal infrastructure needed to accommodate the influx of new people into the area. Would Alpac's taxes in fact cover the costs? Would county residents face an increase in their already high property taxes? How would such an increase affect those on fixed incomes?

> The County Council feels that tax money from the mill will give them a big surplus, and that local taxes will fall. The way I see it, more schools and roads will be required and taxes will likely go up. Fort McMurray, for example, has had ample development during the last few years, but they also have the highest property taxes in Alberta. (Ted Pitman, Prosperity: 7165)

The population of the Athabasca area had been stagnant for at least a decade, and many people had left Athabasca for Edmonton, just 150 kilometres to the south. Local politicians and mill proponents believed that the influx of population would save their dying communities. They assumed that pulp-mill employees would live in the local area and spend their wages in the local economy. No one questioned this assumption, until a Review Board member from the Athabasca area asked Gerry Fenner about the consequences of shift work:

> This mill, if it operates . . . a person [at the mill] would work three days in a row, 12 hours a day; is that right? . . . [I]f you were a family man and had your children attending school in the City of Edmonton . . . and if you had the opportunity to work in the mill a three-day shift with four days off, would you live in Athabasca, Grassland, Lac La Biche . . . is it a possibility that many of the workers working in the mill would, in fact, not live in this area? . . . [T]he impact in terms of jobs for this area may not be anywhere near as high as predicted. (Ted West, Athabasca: 2582-2584)

The terms of reference of the Review Board required it to examine socio-economic impacts, which include numbers and types of jobs and effects on taxes. The governments and the company promoted the economic benefits of the mill, yet, early on in the hearings, the public made Board members aware that no cost-benefit analysis of the project had been done. One environmentalist contended that:

> [A] careful examination of the socio-economic aspects of the proposal should be a top priority . . . because if [jobs] are not there . . . it seems highly unlikely to me that we would even contemplate approving [the mill] because of the benefits that the industry would bring to the environment. (Barry Johnstone, Prosperity: 3870)

The issue, however, went beyond the simple absence of a job and cost-benefit study, to the apparent neglect of socio-economic impacts in the EIA process:

> [I]f there had been proper EARP [Environmental Assessment and Review Process] scoping sessions, we might have seen 20 professional social scientists here from the federal government, as we saw natural scientists this morning. It would have been . . . a recognition that socio-economic impact issues are just as important a study, and the communities need as much assistance in coming to understand what this project's impacts might be as the assistance they need in understanding the impacts on the water, air and wildlife. (Mike Gismondi, Athabasca: 2959)

> How can we determine whether and by how much economic benefits outweigh costs if we are not given a cost breakdown with explanations of the figures? I have read that the forest industry is now a net drain on the BC economy. I'm in no position to judge whether this is correct, but I think we must satisfy ourselves on this point. We have been led to believe that there will be great . . . economic benefit to be had from this project with no hard figures. (Mary Richardson, Athabasca: 3461)

The Board commissioned an independent study of local economic impacts, and concluded:

> Some of the economic benefits and some of the costs were estimated by Alberta-Pacific or other participants. However,

there was no cost-benefit analysis submitted to the Review Board, and the information received is insufficient to allow preparation of an overall cost-benefit study. Any such study would have to include the timber harvesting operations which are beyond the mandate of the Board. (Review Board Report: 54-55)

The Review Board's inability to prepare a comprehensive cost-benefit study underscored the inadequacy of its mandate, which excluded an examination of effects of timber harvesting operations. Thus, the public was given no evidence, even of a comparative nature, that there would be a net economic benefit in return for the tax money being spent to attract the mill, and for the use of public resources.

In this chapter, we have listened to local people who were critical of claims made in Alpac's EIA. When they questioned Alpac's claims, they were questioning more than numbers. They were questioning the company's honesty, its neighbourliness, and the authority of expertise itself. Because company officials were treated by local governments and mill boosters as honoured guests who were bringing the gift of economic well-being to the region, critics had to violate rules of country etiquette to ask tough, public, and sometimes embarrassing questions of these guests. Their questioning revealed how important it is to have detailed knowledge of local conditions in order to predict with assurance what the effects of a large industrial project will be. Critics pushed at the limits of environmental impact assessment as it is now practised by asking questions about the effects of certain factors when considered together, rather than in isolation, and by asking for a more serious socio-economic impact assessment than is usually done.

Although we have focused in this chapter on criticisms of the pulp-mill project, local opinion was deeply divided on whether the mill would or would not benefit the region. Those who thought that it would often focused on the jobs that would be created for local people, and argued, at least implicitly, that economic well-being justified a certain amount of environmental degradation. In the next chapter, we follow the debate among local people about the idea that there is necessarily a tradeoff between creating jobs and protecting the environment.[17]

Notes

1. All items identified as "Filed Documents" are written submissions to the Alpac EIA Review Board, a collection of the Filed Documents is housed in the Athabasca University Library; quotations from the Alberta-Pacific EIA Review Board public hearings are from J. G. Moore and Associates Ltd., *The Alberta-Pacific Environment Impact Assessment Review Board Public Hearing Proceedings, Volumes 1-55* (Edmonton, Alberta: J. G. Moore and Associates Ltd., 1989).

2. Follow-up interview with hearings presenter Jack Van Camp, Fort Smith, NWT. September 1992.

3. Michael McDonald, "Ethics Versus Expertise: The Politics of Technology," in Jorge Nef, Jokelee Vanderkop and Henry Wiseman, eds., *Ethics and Technology: Ethical Choices in the Age of Pervasive Technology,* (Toronto: Wall and Thompson, 1989), pp. 119-124. Quotations in this paragraph are from page 120.

4. See, for example, Chapter 3, "Authority," in Barry Barnes, *About Science* (Oxford: Blackwell, 1985).

5. This and all further citations of the Alpac Written Responses in this chapter refer to Alberta-Pacific Forest Industries Inc., *Alberta-Pacific Forest Industries Inc.*, *Written Submissions and Responses, Volumes 1, 2 and 3* (Edmonton, Alberta: Alberta-Pacific Forest Industries Inc., 1989) The item cited here is the Response to Emil Zachkewich, Question 14, p. 47.

6. See Environment Canada, *A Report on Canada's Progress Towards a National Set of Environmental Indicators,* SOE Report 91-1 (Ottawa: Minister of Supply and Services Canada, 1991), pp. iv, 64, 72-76. This report is the result of a project mandated by the federal Green Plan to identify "national environmental indicators which are consistent, reliable indicators to measure the quality of our environment." Environmental indicators are to be used for "translating quantities of environmental data into succinct information that can . . . be used by decision makers and the general public." The authors of the report argue that "we cannot look to traditional economic indicators in assessing the importance of the environment to our individual and collective future . . . reliance on economic indicators can distort the environmental reality in which we live." One of the environmental indicators identified and discussed in the report is the loss of agricultural land.

7. This and all further citiations of the Alpac EIA Main Report in this chapter refer to Alberta-Pacific Forest Industries Inc., *Alberta-Pacific Forest Industries Inc. Environmental Impact Assessment Bleached Kraft Pulp Mill Main Report* (Edmonton, Alberta: Alberta-Pacific Forest Industries Inc., 1989).

8. This and all further citations of the Review Board Report in this chapter refer to Alberta-Pacific Environmental Impact Assessment Review Board, *The Proposed Alberta-Pacific Pulp Mill: Report of the EIA Review Board,* March 1990 (Edmonton, Alberta: Alberta Environment, 1990). The quotation cited here occurs on p. 56.

9. Review Board Report: 56.
10. Alpac EIA Main Report: Appendix 5, p. 3.11.
11. Alpac Written Responses: 88.
12. John Ashworth, Prosperity: 3936-3937.
13. Alpac EIA Main Report: Appendix 7, pp. 7.1-7.3.
14. Alberta-Pacific Forest Industries Inc., *Alberta-Pacific Forest Industries Inc., Environmental Impact Assessment Supplemental Information,* Edmonton, Alberta: Alberta-Pacific Forest Industries Inc.) p. 111.
15. Letter from Highway 620 Advocates, Prosperity: 7556.
16. See Filed Document I-2.
17. This chapter draws from a study funded by CIDA's Canada-Asia Partnership, "Community Environmental Indicators: A Case Study of the Alpac EIA Hearings," Joan Sherman and Michael Gismondi, January 1992, 116 pp. An earlier version of this chapter was read at the Learned Societies Annual Meetings, Charlottetown, PEI, May 1992, for the Canadian Association for Studies in International Development session on "Breaking Out of the Orthodoxy: Academics, Development Workers and the Discourse of Sustainability, Participation and Equity."

"The job creation story is just a ploy."
(Alex Makar, area farmer, Filed Document O-162)
(Photograph of pulp-mill rally, courtesy of *The Athabasca Advocate*)

CHAPTER 7

Jobs, Jobs, Jobs

Thank You for a Future for Our Children. (Sign at pulp mill rally)

[B]eing an industrial country with resources to tap, we must pursue these avenues to maintain our standard of living and are fortunate to have this opportunity to develop these resources by companies such as Alpac. . . . I sincerely believe that a good environment is a healthy economic one. (Douglas Blatt, Athabasca, Filed Document G-48: 2, 4)[1]

We are living today in a world that is showing increasing signs of stress in the environment, stress at such a level that we can no longer afford to ignore it. So it is within this environmental context that we must address the issues of high unemployment and the need for economic diversity, and try to achieve both while maintaining a balance with the environment. Alpac's bleached kraft pulp mill does not provide a good balance between jobs and the environment. . . . With this bleached kraft pulp mill proposal we are being given a choice between jobs and environment. What kind of a choice is that? Certainly, not a fair one. It's like telling someone they can either have a pair of lungs or a heart, but they can't have both. We need both to survive, lungs and heart, environment and jobs. (Merilyn Peruniak, Athabasca: 3314)

Merilyn Peruniak wanted to address issues of unemployment and economic diversity in the context of an environment under stress. Alpac and the provincial and local governments resisted. They emphasized the economic environment and job creation, arguing that the project would provide training and jobs for the young and the unemployed, remove natives from the welfare rolls, and increase economic opportunities in northern Alberta.[2]

In his December 1988 speech announcing approval in principle of the Alpac mill, Premier Getty declared that, "[The mill] will contribute significantly to the economic development of northern Alberta [and] will create 1300 direct jobs, with major economic spinoffs. An additional 2600 indirect jobs will be created by the project."[3] Six months later, the discussion of job creation in the newly released Alpac EIA gave the same message. Alpac presented its employment opportunities in glowing, if somewhat mystifying, terms: "estimated direct employment in the primary impact region during construction of the pulp mill will be 33,600 man-months over three years. . . . In addition some 5,040 man-months of indirect employment are expected."[4]

Using "appropriate economic multipliers" Alpac predicted that construction-related employment for all of Alberta (including the primary impact region) would be 80,400 man-months, and for Canada as a whole 114,000 man-months. It also estimated total direct and indirect employment for the Athabasca/Lac La Biche region at 1050 jobs, and in the overall region, 1,925 jobs.[5] The lure of hundreds of direct jobs and countless indirect construction and spin-off jobs was now tangible, and critics who questioned the economics or raised environmental concerns were portrayed by the establishment as unrealistic and as posing a threat to the unemployed.

The rhetoric of spin-off jobs, and direct-jobs, and the calculations in man-months magnified Alpac's job impact in the minds of some members of the public, but others remained skeptical. Emil Zachkewich, a local farmer critical of Alpac's pitch, drew attention to the way the EIA was written:

> [T]he entire EIA documentation is designed something like a "sales catalogue." The emphasis on economic benefits to the surrounding urban centres is in detail and very specific. On the other hand, the environmental concerns of the mill site community are addressed with such terms as "minimal," "negligible," "not expected," "do not foresee," "no research available," etc. (Alpac Written Responses: 28)[6]

Another mill site resident, Betty Sewall, criticized Alpac's manner of responding to questions about its EIA:

[T]here have been economic questions and environmental questions [to Alpac]. Those of an economic nature appear to have been addressed [by Alpac] with dialogue, extensive support, immediacy and cooperation. Those questions of an environmental nature have been addressed with avoidance, suspicion, vagueness, procrastination, and confrontation. (Alpac Written Responses: 115)

Just as it was difficult to be opposed to the rhetoric of sustainable development, so it was equally difficult to oppose the rhetoric of job creation. Nevertheless, many people rejected the job creation claims of the government and the company. This chapter explores five aspects of the debate about jobs: using the promise of jobs for members of area families as a means of promoting the mill, unions and workplace health, jobs for natives, the political economy of logging, and job creation alternatives.

Job Creation: For the Children, For the Family

This mill will allow an opportunity to have our younger generation stay and work in our area, rather than move to larger urban centres. Of major importance to any individual or family is the ability to provide for ourselves and our families. (Walter Harrynuck, Mayor of the Village of Boyle, Prosperity: 7456)

I have some sympathy for the youth who cannot find work locally. I had to leave my home town to find employment. Still I would rather have had that than have my children grow up in the shadow of a mill that was poisoning the environment. Or having a son die of cancer in a mill town (as a friend of mine did). (Peter Holt)[7]

With Alberta's farming economy in decline, economic proposals that promise to revive rural communities feed into the discourse of "recovering the past"—a golden past of self-sufficient farms and self-reliant communities. The sacred mantra "for the family," when combined with Alberta's prevailing neo-conservative ideology, became one of the potent messages used to promote forestry development. For example, in a speech to a northern chamber of commerce, Fred McDougall, the Deputy Minister, Forestry, Lands and Wildlife, said that the government was doing more than making jobs, it was preserving the family, because "increased job opportunities will mean that more families will be able to stay together."[8]

At the hearings, some farmers from Athabasca county told the Review Board that agriculture could no longer provide their families with adequate incomes, and that they believed the pulp mill would provide a stable economic future for the region and perhaps jobs for their children:

> Farming is a great life. We love it, but it is getting harder and harder to keep the wolf away from the door. I know for a fact that many of the people who are strongly opposed to the mill have off-farm income. More and more farmers must go out to work in order to meet the pressing commitments on the farm. With the mill here, we will be closer to home, to our families, and still be able to supplement our farm incomes. (Doris Stewart, Prosperity: 7250)

> As a family of seven living near the site of the proposed pulp mill, we are excited about this much needed and long awaited development. . . . As it stands now the outlook is very bleak for the younger generation as job prospects are basically non-existent. The farming situation is getting worse all the time. At least 90% of the farmers in our area have their income supplemented with off-farm jobs either by the husband or wife, or as in our case, both of us.
> (Marion and Janet Kanarek, Boyle, Filed Document O-129)

Stewart and the Kanareks supported the Alpac project as a way of helping farmers and their children. However, at recent public hearings on the future of the family farm, politicians had received quite different recommendations from farmers, recommendations that involved stabilizing the agricultural economy, preventing farm foreclosures and evictions, and helping young people stay on the land. One farm woman condemned the government for proposing a pulp mill instead:

For these same leaders to come forth into the heart of our agricultural community and tell us they have come to save us from a life of poverty and ruin by bringing us a multi-national giant to employ us in a stinking factory, I can only guess this to be the epitome of this government's misunderstanding of the people who live on the land. (Janice Pitman, Athabasca: 3052-3053)

Many families who farmed close to the mill felt as Pitman did. They believed that governments were willing to sacrifice farms in Prosperity to make jobs for townspeople or for farmers farther away. Support for the mill as a major source of employment was stronger in the local towns than in the farming community surrounding the mill site. For example, the mayor of Plamondon stated:

[M]any of our senior citizens are speaking favourably of this project because it means that their children and grandchildren that have had to leave the area to find employment may now have a chance at working close to family and friends. (Elaine G. Gauthier, Filed Document O-169)

Michelle Plante, a young woman who actively promoted the pulp mill through Friends of the Mill, and who helped to organize a mill booster rally at the proposed mill site, felt that the opportunity for local employment was a strong factor in favour of the mill:

I have moved away from Athabasca, away from my entire friends and family in hope of finding a career because there is nothing left in Athabasca, unfortunately, for the younger generation, other than gas pumps and grocery store clerks. That's sad, but that is the truth. . . . I am concerned about the environment. I'm young, and I have many more years to breathe this air and live in this environment. I may some day as well bring children into this world and will have the same concerns for them. However, I don't want to see them have to struggle in life either. To make a career for themselves or to find their place in life, to find a job, I don't want to see them suffer as I am and a lot of my peers are as well . . . on behalf of my generation and the generations to come, and the unemployed out there, please give it another serious thought. (Fort McMurray: 243-245)

Some of the young people in Athabasca did not accept without reservation the rhetoric of "jobs for our children, jobs to keep families together." They wanted to be consulted about decisions that would affect their future:

> We are the future that so many people on both sides of the Alpac pulp mill issue are worried about. One side is trying to destroy the future for us; the other side doesn't want to bother building it. Until this time, however, no one has bothered with our opinions or concerns. . . . We have no problem with the economic benefits this community would gain from investments such as a pulp mill, but are very worried about the environment. (Doug Nazaruk, Edwin Parr Composite High School, Athabasca: 3179)

The hearings in downstream communities placed the theme of job creation and working near home, family and friends, in a different light. The Review Board was reminded that the issue of jobs was not a simple one of job creation around the mill site. While some people were getting jobs, other people, in other locations, could be losing them. In Fort Resolution, NWT, there was a concern that the livelihood of youth in the north could be destroyed if the pulp mill were approved. One student made the point this way:

> We, the young, have the rights to speak and express feelings regarding our future . . . this proposed pulp mill may destroy our livelihood and future forever. As you are all aware, a community this small can only provide a limited amount of jobs. With the possibility of destroying our lands, waters, no jobs or cash compensation will ever replace the damage that will be done to our lands and future. (Karen Lafferty, Deninoo Community School, Fort Resolution: 3557)

Jobs at What Cost: Worker Health

> A further environmental issue that is often overlooked in
> hearings of this kind is the question of health and safety in
> the pulp mill itself. Kraft pulp mills are dangerous places to
> work. Many toxic chemicals are used in the process and
> hundreds of others are produced as byproducts. . . . The
> harmful effects of these chemicals range from allergic
> reactions to the incidence of cancer higher than that of the
> general population. (David Coles, Canadian Paperworkers
> Union: Athabasca 3250-3251)

> [W]e are not aware of any adverse health effects for the long
> term employees of pulp mills in BC or Sweden. (Alpac,
> Written Responses: 55)[9]

The Canadian Paperworkers Union (CPU) presented a sobering
message to those who anticipated mill jobs for their children: these
jobs may pose a risk to their children's health. In 1989, the CPU was
a national industrial union of some 72,000 members. Dave Coles,
the Alberta organizer, and Keith Neuman, the national research
officer, read a prepared text from the CPU national leadership that
questioned the appropriateness of chlorine bleaching in Alpac's
proposed mill. Their brief emphasized that they spoke on behalf of
people who have first-hand work experience inside pulp and paper
bleaching plants. The CPU believed that health problems among its
members and evidence of environmental pollution downstream
from mills indicated that chlorine bleaching should be phased out
in existing plants, and that no new plants using this process should
be built.

> David Schindler (Review Board member): So is this not
> tantamount to endorsing that the occupation that your
> members hold be rendered extinct?

> Dave Coles: Well, I guess we have to face the realities of life.
> I'll use for an example when people worked in asbestos
> mines and were assured it was good for their health, they
> ended up with problems and had to make changes. We as a
> union, and us as a society, are having to wrestle with a lot of

these environmental issues brought to fruition in the last years. There is problems with pulp and paper, and we appreciate that. (Athabasca: 3261)

Gerry Fenner (Alpac Vice President, Pulp): [A]re you going to not try to organize this mill because of your concern about the environment?

Coles: [W]e'd never disassociate ourselves from any class of worker, whether it's in this pulp mill or any other.

Keith Neuman: We believe that workers should be represented by unions everywhere, no matter whether we think the project that they are working on is ideal or not. So that's kind of an irrelevant question. (Athabasca: 3275-3276)

The CPU's intervention challenged two public discourses often heard since the mill was announced. The first was that industrial workers were anti-environmentalists, because environmentalists threatened their jobs. The CPU representatives spoke at the invitation of Friends of the Athabasca, and their intervention indicated that pulp mill workers are willing to work with environmentalists to promote environmentally sound development. Secondly, by showing that mill jobs themselves posed a health hazard for mill workers, the CPU speakers weakened the argument that the proposed mill would solve the employment problems of northern Albertans and their children.

This presentation, made from the perspective of workers on the shop floor, sensitized the Review Board and the general public to increasing health concerns about chlorine bleaching of pulp. Furthermore, it made it clear that the union put the interests of workers ahead of its corporate interest in recruiting members and preserving the kraft pulping profession. This attitude contrasted with Alpac's willingness to risk workers' health to make a profit.

Jobs for Natives: Promises, Commitments, Past Practice

Alberta-Pacific will encourage Native participation wherever it is practicable, taking into account project requirements, scheduling and cost considerations, and capabilities of Native residents and Native businesses. Wherever the

capability exists or could reasonably be developed for a
Native resident or Native business to compete for a Project
opportunity, special efforts will be made to assist them in
participating. (Alpac EIA Main Report: Appendix 6, 4.1: 6.10)

When they [forestry companies] came into our areas and
wanted to expand and acquire timber permits and build
mills, they made many promises to us, but there are very
few Indian people employed in these mills in western
Alberta. Consequently, if these promises from Alberta-
Pacific are going to be meaningful, you should make sure
that they are generous, specific and firmly bound to them.
(Chief Johnsen Sewepagaham, Little Red River Band, Fort
Chipewyan: 1445)

I go down to Port Alberni where there is three mills, one of
those being a major pulp mill . . . hundreds of employees.
. . . In that pulp mill there, if I had three fingers on one
hand, I could count the amount of Indian people that are
working in those pulp mills. So it has never, ever meant any
monetary gain for our people. (Chief Simon Lucas,
Wabasca: 6030)

Politicians and Alpac promoted the mill to the public by
claiming that it would make jobs for natives. MLA Mike Cardinal
explained the native position this way: "[T]he Native people told me
one thing plain. They are sick of welfare; they want an alternative to
the welfare system; they want economic development."[10] Alpac
anticipated that the majority of employment opportunities for
native people would occur in the forestry operations.

It was difficult to determine how many forestry jobs would
actually be created by the project, let alone ascertain how many
jobs would go to natives. Alpac stated in its EIA that there would be
660 "full-time equivalent"[11] jobs supplying wood to the mill. Six
months later, at the EIA hearings, Alpac revealed that only 35 of
these jobs would be full-time Alpac forestry positions. The other
625 jobs would go to independent log haulers, logging contractors,
or loggers working for contractors, and they would be seasonal.

All we heard about was jobs, full-time jobs. We didn't even
hear the definition of "full-time equivalent job" until last

night . . . [now we learn] it's about 750 jobs for three winter
months, twenty-four hours a day, seven days a week; and 400
some odd jobs for four months, five days a week, in the
summer . . . not necessarily the same jobs and not necessarily the same people. . . . I called it "Maritime
development" where jobs are subsidized by taxpayers
through the UIC system. (Mike Gismondi, Athabasca: 2558-
2559, 2964-2965)

Residents of Janvier, a native community close enough to Alpac's
timber harvesting activities to benefit from logging jobs, were
concerned with issues of land claims, trapping and hunting rights,
native identity, and traditional ways of life, yet they did not reject
the Alpac mill. They wanted to be included in Alpac's plans, and
they wanted to log:

The Janvier Indian Band is not against the pulp mill
development and FMA but concerned that the community
derive direct and indirect economic and social benefits
from the development, particularly in the timber harvesting
operations. (Marvin McDonald, Janvier: 620)

While members of the Janvier community were interested in economic development that was compatible with traditional life-styles,
they were equally concerned to get solid commitments from Alpac:

[We] don't want to lose our traditional way of life, but still, I
think we can work with Alpac and the industry in this area
and still maintain our livelihood. . . . [W]hat we would like
with Alpac is . . . a comprehensive written agreement . . .
regarding training, employment, business opportunities,
joint forest management, support and services.
(Chief Walter Janvier, Janvier: 629)

In addition to agreements for joint forest management, the Band
wanted minimum quotas for native employment and training:

There is concern that Alpac policies and practices will make
some of the residents ineligible. Mill jobs require grade 12
entrance levels for employment, requirement to own capital
intensive logging equipment in stump-to-dump contracts.

We recommend that Alpac be required . . . to have logging contractors hire at least 15 to 20 per cent native employees, and have something in there that gives us some assurance that this will take place. (Marvin McDonald, Janvier: 623-624)

Alpac's Gerry Fenner was guarded in his response to such demands:

[At] this point in this project we have been dealing with essentially the process. And when we developed our Native Affairs policy, I was concerned that this policy be developed to handle process and not substance and substance really has not been addressed by us, and I know that the kind of concerns that you brought up today deal with the substance and not particularly the process. . . . [W]e at this point do not have any agreement to proceed with this development . . . so it's very difficult . . . to sit down at tables and negotiate the kind of substance that I know that you want. . . . [I]t is your kind of community that this company is committed to helping. (Janvier: 644-645)

This elusive response raised concerns among Review Board members:

Mr. Fenner, if I might raise one matter before we ask the Chief and the others. Sir, it seems to me that we're sitting here as a panel and we hear the Janvier delegation saying that we need something of substance before Alpac or any other party should be given a go ahead. And I think, and I hope you'll both correct me if I'm wrong, but I think I hear Alpac saying if we get a go ahead, we'll address the matters of substance, and it seems that we're simply on different planes here. (Gerry DeSorcy, Review Board chairman, Janvier: 661)

Many natives distrusted Alpac because they had heard many times before that substance would be dealt with after projects were approved. Some speakers offered evidence of industry's failures to provide employment for natives:

While stating they are committed to ensure employment and business opportunities for native people, corporations rarely make the hard decisions, invest the kind of resources, or institute the policies and programs to make this commitment a reality. The five Bands in the Fort McMurray area are very familiar with the promises of the proponents of mega-projects to provide training, employment and business opportunities for native people. We are also very familiar with broken promises and lack of significant benefits, jobs and businesses for native people that continue to plague our region. (Chief Robert Cree, Athabasca Tribal Council, Janvier: 671)

I interviewed the union representative [from Alpac's parent company] who we heard speak here on Saturday night. I asked him how many Native people worked in the [Crestbrook] mill. . . . He told me the mill union has 220 members, there is one Native person that works in that mill. (Mike Gismondi, Athabasca: 2963)

Since 1960 the Canfor sawmill has been operating in the High Level area. It provides permanent employment for 300 people, plus 500 jobs during the logging season. The sawmill employs 200 truckers, purchases $22 million worth of logs from local contractors yearly. No Dene Tha are hired at the mill. They are offered the odd seasonal bush-clearing contract. (Father Camille Piché, Fort Chipewyan: 1454)

Chief Robert Cree perceived Alpac's reluctance to make commitments as a double standard:

Alpac wants contractual commitments to cut timber on our traditional lands and wants the precise terms and conditions of their commitments and obligations spelled out. We as native people want no less a commitment. We no longer believe in the good faith commitments of companies and their senior management without these being clarified in writing and put in contractual arrangements such as the FMA spelling out the respective obligations of both parties. (Chief Robert Cree, Athabasca Tribal Council, Janvier: 674)

Chief Sewepagaham argued that even contractual arrangements, as in forest management agreements, would prove inadequate for his Little Red River Band, because native people would lose control over the forest resource. He questioned the value of a developmental strategy that necessitated that natives supply their wage labour to an outside corporation. Rather, he counselled that native communities must exercise collective authority over forest resources to maintain their independence:

> [The Alpac FMA] is bad for Native people. . . . [I]t removes this very important, and often only resource from being used for development of local economies. Our community has tried to get allocations of timber resources for local sawmills and other purposes which will be locally controlled, owned and managed and employ a large number of Native people in proper forestry practices. . . . In giving away the forests to these other companies, we lose control of the forests surrounding our communities and are left to wage jobs, if any jobs at all. (Chief Johnsen Sewepagaham, Fort Chipewyan: 1444)

The Political Economy of Logging

> [W]ealth and jobs are coming uncoupled . . . today wealth is increasingly created by capital, by robots and computers, not labour . . . multifunctional machines . . . in the bush are coming fast. Automation is working its way through the mills. So if jobs are the lure for any new development, view the prophetic figures sceptically. (J. Stanley Rowe)[12]

All logging is becoming more mechanized. There is no more chain saw work. These mills are planning on using heavy machinery such as a feller-buncher. Each machine costs up to 1/2 million dollars and causes horrible damage to the environment. The new machinery . . . require less people since a 3-man crew can replace a regular 13-man chain saw and skidder operation. (Chief Charles Beaver, Bigstone Band, Wabasca, Filed Document O-145: 4)

Chief Beaver's concerns are confirmed by studies of changes in logging practices in New Brunswick.[13] The chain-saw/skidder model of logging, used in that province until the early 1970s, was labour intensive. A skilled worker would cut a trail or area of trees with a chain saw, delimb them, buck them to length for yarding to the roadside and loading onto trucks, and perform his own equipment maintenance. Now, logging operations seldom employ workers to cut trees with chain saws or to work with skidders and loaders. These skilled tradespeople have been displaced by the mechanized feller-buncher which does all these jobs, and also grasps the trees into large bunches for loading, with one or two workers—"there is what amounts to an assembly line in the woods operating twenty-four hours per day, as required by the large amount of capital investment."[14]

Father Camille Piché noted similar trends in forestry in Alberta:

The Northwest Economic Initiatives study . . . points out that, "In the logging and sawmill industry, there is a strong move towards greater reliance on high tech equipment to increase productivity per man day and to lower operating costs. This means that the existing work force is shrinking and the skill level of the employees is rising." Guess where that will leave us? With an average Grade 3 level of schooling, people in Assumption face a bleak prospect for employment, indeed. At present, 48 persons are full-time employees of the Footner Lake forest management. Not one is Dene Tha. Some Dene Tha have seasonal work fighting forest fires in the summer. Others pick acorns in the fall which are used by Canfor for reseeding. Dene are not squirrels. If the Dene Tha are to participate with dignity in forest management, they require at least a 10-year moratorium on pulp mills in the area. (Fort Chipewyan: 1464-1465)

As logging becomes mechanized, the gap widens not only between the existing skills of the workers and those needed to run the machines in the bush, but also between the capital needed to purchase these machines and the credit ratings of native communities. Piché's call for a moratorium paralleled the position of many clergy who, during the Mackenzie Valley pipeline debate, saw structural obstacles to native employment.[15]

A professional forester and former forestry manager did not agree that a moratorium was desirable:

> Religious mentors to the aboriginal people tell the historical story of life for the bands accurately and passionately. . . . Reverend Camille Piché is a perfect example. . . . But the request of Father Piché to stall aboriginal people's employment for 10 years, while they get trained, is illogical. The people need employment and income now. The development proposals can meet the NEED now. Native people can be quickly made employable if they are motivated and encouraged to shed the habit of indolence and accepted poverty—by giving them a concrete, visible alternative. I have experienced this kind of opportunity and have made it work. (James D. Clark, Registered Professional Forester and consultant, Filed Document O-137: 5)

In contrast, Chief Marcel of the Athabasca Tribal Council asked the Review Board to consider the advantages of a moratorium for careful planning, second thought, and firm commitments:

> We would ask the Board to consider the advantages of the moratorium proposed by the ATC [Athabasca Tribal Council]. . . . A moratorium would also allow native communities time to get ready for the development, get government funding in place, get management and socio-economic agreements signed, and to get appropriate timber quotas and Forestry Management Agreements in place. We have no hope or confidence this will be done once the permit is given . . . if Alberta Pacific is not here for a fast buck on a fast track, on their terms, but interested in long-term environmental opportunities in Alberta, they should not object to a moratorium. The trees will not go away, and neither will we. It is our lives, our economy, our health, our communities that are at risk for their profit. (Prosperity: 7242-7243)

Opportunity Costs and Job Alternatives

[We] believe this whole project has been sold to the public in an inappropriate way. The basic misconception is that there are only two alternatives for northern Alberta: a bleached kraft pulp mill or no development. . . . [W]hat are the other ways we could develop the north beside a kraft pulp mill . . . we should be looking at the economic alternatives as well as the environmental impact.. . . . [W]e thought that the Board should consider the impact of a mill on alternative, existing and future economic developments when assessing the total pros and cons of the Alpac mill. In other words, we wanted the Board to look at opportunity costs. (Peter Holt, Prosperity: 7196, 7197)

Most people speaking for the environment were not, as their opponents suggested, against development and job creation. They were concerned, however, that alternatives to a bleached kraft pulp mill had not been seriously considered, and that job creation in the pulp sector could mean lost opportunities and even job losses in other sectors. As we have seen, this issue was particularly significant to northern residents:

[T]he people in northern Alberta, Yukon and Northwest Territories all depend upon the fishing and trapping and tourism for their employment. We are too far north to be employed at these pulp mills. What will we do when our industries are wiped out? Are you willing to buy our groceries and pay our rent? (Kimberley Gusek, Prosperity: 7484)

Northern residents argued that the opportunity costs of the mill might be higher than most people thought. Dan Creurer told the Review Board that there were 42 fishermen and "in excess of 300 people who benefit in one way or another from the commercial fishery in Fort Chipewyan."[16] Creurer read off the income figures for the fishermen's association over several years. He noted that in two years they had had no revenue, and explained to the Review Board why this loss had occurred:

We all know that tainted fish means an end to the fisheries industry in Lake Athabasca. The zero figures that I read . . . for income in 1982 and in 1983 were a direct consequence of the oil spill by Suncor in 1981. Our fisheries were shut down for two years because the fish were tainted. This is a very vivid example, a very easy example of what can happen when fish are tainted. Nobody wants them. If nobody wants them, forget it, fisheries is dead. (Dan Creurer, Delta Native Fishermen's Association, Fort Chipewyan: 1398-1399)

Other northerners feared that their livelihood from tourism would suffer a loss as a result of logging and pollution. Tourism is the third-largest economic sector in Alberta, generating $2 billion per year. Peter Holt questioned both the effect the mill would have on present and future tourism revenues, and whether the mill was the best economic venture for the region:

[B]y the year 2000, the Minister of Alberta Tourism has projected it will be a $10 billion industry. . . . It's not something to be kind of cast aside. Within tourism, there is a growing trend to eco-tourism and wilderness experiences. More and more people want a holiday where they can go to some place that is natural, untouched by industry. . . . [T]here is going to be a real impact on that industry [tourism] from the Alpac mill. . . . Above and beyond the actual physical impacts, there is going to be the psychological impact of the pulp mill on tourists. (Prosperity: 7198)

Confronted by concerns that the mill would interfere with potential growth in tourism, Alpac fought back by presenting the mill as a tourist attraction and a tourist agent:

Alberta-Pacific will work with Travel Alberta and Tourism Action Committees of the various municipalities to help promote the area as a tourist destination. This can be done by making tourist information available to businessmen visiting the mill and to those participating in mill tours. (Alpac EIA, Supplemental Information: 106)[17]

> In terms of pulp mill towns not being tourist attractions, Alberta-Pacific does not agree. . . . . Tourism actually has benefitted from the forest industry in the Kootenays as more money is available for recreation facilities and other amenities. (Alpac Written Responses: 66-67)[18]

A northern tourist industry representative, Oliver Glanfield, countered Alpac's positive tourism image, "[S]everal of our current tourism staff in Fort Chipewyan have worked in other areas of Canada where pulp mills have resulted in a depressed tourism market."[19] Mike Freeland, of the Travel Industry Association of NWT, told the Review Board that in a recent survey of Northwest Territories tourist lodge operators working with fishing or naturalist lodges, two respondents mentioned that they had been "'pulped out of business' in Ontario," and had "headed north to the last frontier to get away from it all."[20]

Recycling was another alternative to the pulp mill suggested by many presenters. Citizens criticized the government for offering Alpac public money to locate in Alberta when what was needed was a mill to recycle paper. Dave Hubert, speaking for the Mennonite Central Committee Alberta, the Citizens for Public Justice, and the Edmonton Recycling Centre, told the Review Board that his organization ran the Edmonton recycling program which processed 6000 tonnes of used paper in 1989. Hubert wanted to harvest the "urban forest" of paper wasted annually in Alberta landfills or disposed of in other "non-productive or even environmentally destructive ways." He estimated that a curbside recycling collection system would create 300 or more jobs: "In fact, the interest on the Alberta Government loan to Alberta-Pacific would, we believe, be more than enough to implement a high quality curbside recycling program across Alberta."[21]

Development is often promoted by weighing the benefits to the economy from the creation of jobs against any possible environmental effects. This type of discussion is known as the "jobs versus environment" trade-off. In the case of Alpac, mill supporters and the government suggested that a framework existed to weigh economic growth and job creation against the value of environmental protection, and that, within this framework, the Alpac proposal had been judged satisfactory. The Athabasca Chamber of Commerce, for example, declared that the massive infusion of capital ($1.3 billion) and the many jobs should outweigh environmental concerns:

> The point of view of the Chamber is that the benefits to the public good and the advancement of social and economic factors in the region and province will far outweigh any possible adverse environmental concerns. (Phil Rowlands, Athabasca Chamber of Commerce, Athabasca: 2921-2922)

At the hearings it became clear, however, that the jobs side of the jobs-environment equation was complex, and needed to be examined as thoroughly and rigorously as the environment side. Examples of development alternatives, such as tourism and recycling, challenged the job creation discourse in two ways. First, such alternatives addressed in dollars and cents how Canadian entrepreneurs could create environmentally friendly jobs and improve the environment, with less government investment than that given to transnationals such as Alpac. Second, public intervention raised consciousness about the "jobs versus jobs" trade-off that was occurring.

The mayor of the downstream community of Fort Smith expressed the sentiments of most northerners when he challenged another side of the "jobs versus environment" equation, arguing that no calculation had been done of the environmental price of the jobs that would be created by the mill: "[E]verybody recognized there was an environmental price, but they didn't try to do a balance sheet to show why it was necessary to pay that price."[22]

Finally, whether or not a jobs-environment balance sheet had been created and audited, there were participants who rejected the premise that the environment could be traded off for jobs:

> [E]arth is our mother. We do not accept the view that injury to the land is justified by jobs and business opportunities that result. The land is our security and perennial provider, and it remains our paramount concern. (Ralph Makokis, Beaver Lake: 1295)

In the next chapter, we reveal the final position of the Review Board, and how its conclusions were sidestepped by people who did not believe, as did Steven Norn, a Grade 8 student from Deninoo

School, that "the environment is more important than paper, money and jobs."[23]

Notes

1. All items identified as "Filed Documents" are written submissions to the Alpac EIA Review Board, a collection of the Filed Documents is housed in the Athabasca University Library; quotations from the Alberta-Pacific EIA Review Board public hearings are from J. G. Moore and Associates Ltd., *The Alberta-Pacific Environment Impact Assessment Review Board Public Hearing Proceedings, Volumes 1-55* (Edmonton, Alberta, J. G. Moore and Associates Ltd., 1989).

2. Northern Alberta is an economic hinterland. See the discussion of the hinterland concept in Thomas Dunk, ed., *Social Relations in Resource Hinterlands* (Thunder Bay, Ontario: Lakehead University, Centre for Northern Studies, 1991).

3. Premier Don Getty, Alberta News Release, Government of Alberta. December 13, 1988. Getty released a fact sheet that claimed 1300 direct and approximately 2600 indirect jobs. Weeks later, Alpac revised the numbers downward to 1100 direct jobs and 2200 indirect jobs.

4. This and all further citations of the Alpac EIA Main Report in this chapter refer to Alberta-Pacific Forest Industries Inc., *Alberta-Pacific Forest Industries Inc. Environmental Impact Assessment Bleached Kraft Pulp Mill Main Report* (Edmonton, Alberta: Alberta-Pacific Forest Industries Inc., 1989). This information is contained in Sections 5.3.1.1., 5.3.1.2.

5. Alpac EIA Main Report: Sections 5.3.1.1, 5.3.1.2.

6. This and all further citations of Alpac Written Responses in this chapter refer to Alberta-Pacific Forest Industries Inc., *Alberta-Pacific Forest Industries Inc., Written Submissions and Responses, Volumes 1, 2 and 3* (Edmonton, Alberta: Alberta-Pacific Forest Industries Inc., 1989).

7. Peter Holt, Letter to the Editor, *Athabasca Advertiser*, April 10, 1989.

8. Fred W. McDougall, Deputy Minister, Forestry, Lands and Wildlife, January 21, 1989, Speech to Grande Prairie Chamber of Commerce, p. 12.

9. Alpac Written Responses, Response to submission by Klaas Vink, p. 55.

10. Athabasca-Lac La Biche MLA Mike Cardinal, *The Alberta Government Presentation on the Report of the EIA Review Board on The Proposed Alberta-Pacific Pulp Mill*, Athabasca Community Centre, Athabasca, Alberta, March 2, 1990, p. 15.

11. Alpac EIA Main Report: Appendix 4, Section 3.1.2.

12. J. Stanley Rowe, "The Effects of Pulp Mills on the Environment," *Alpac EIA, Technical Workshop, Bleached Kraft Mill Public Participation Program*, Appendix B, p. 99.

13. Michael Clow, Aloysius Hayes, and Peter MacDonald, "Contrasting Paths of Development in Tree Harvesting Systems on the Miramichi" (Paper delivered at the Canadian Political Science Association: Political Economy Section, Learned Societies Annual Meeting, Charlottetown, PEI, 4 June 1992). The authors address both the technical division of labour in logging and the formal and real subordination of labour to capital in the production process.

14. Michael Clow et al., p. 2.

15. See Roger Hutchinson, *Prophets, Pastors and Public Choices: Canadian Churches and the Mackenzie Valley Pipeline Debate* (Waterloo, Ontario: Wilfrid Laurier University Press, 1992).

16. Dan Creurer, Fort Chipewyan: 1389-1390.

17. Alberta-Pacific Forest Industries Inc., *Alberta-Pacific Forest Industries Inc. Environmental Impact Assessment, Supplemental Information* (Edmonton, Alberta: Alberta-Pacific Forest Industries Inc., 1989).

18. Alpac Written Responses, Response to submission by James O. Darwish, p. 66.

19. Oliver Glanfield, Tourism Committee, Fort Chipewyan: 1369.

20. Mike Freeland, Edmonton: 4353-4354.

21. Dave Hubert, Filed Document N-233.

22. Follow-up interview with hearings presenter Mayor Dennis Bevington, Fort Smith, NWT. September 1992.

23. Stephen Norn, Fort Resolution: 3559.

Announcement to postpone pulp-mill construction
(Photograph courtesy of *The Athabaskan*)

CHAPTER 8

"Political" Science

Allow me to say at the outset that the Government accepts the specific recommendation of the Alberta-Pacific Environmental Impact Assessment Review Board; that the proposed Alberta-Pacific project, as planned, be delayed pending further studies on the Athabasca River.
(Ralph Klein, Minister of Alberta Environment)[1]

My guess is that such studies, given the constraints of expertise available, the number of samples that would have to be taken and analyzed, would [take] several years.
(David Schindler, Review Board member)[2]

You probably know how disappointed I am that this project will be delayed, but I can assure you that I will do everything possible to ensure that this delay does not drag on. I have 100 per cent assurance from the President of Alpac that they are still with us and that they have confidence that the project will proceed in the near future. (Mike Cardinal, MLA, Athabasca-Lac La Biche)[3]

On March 2, 1990, in a packed and tension-filled Athabasca community hall, the Alpac EIA Review Board released its report. Board members were unanimous in their support of the report and its recommendations. They were very proud of their accomplishment, and one Review Board member, Jim Boucher, stated, "Our decision is something we feel we can live with for the rest of our lives."[4]

The Board recommended that the proposed pulp mill not be approved "at this time." While recognizing that the Alpac mill would be "one of the least polluting bleached kraft pulp mills in the world," and "would have economic benefits associated with it," the Board raised concerns about health and environmental effects of dioxins and furans in pulp-mill effluent, and recommended that "further scientific studies on the river systems be conducted to determine if the Alberta-Pacific proposed mill could proceed without serious hazard to life in the river and for downstream users."[5]

The proposed river studies were to include, among other things:

[S]urveys of fish, their habitats, and the food chains that support them; review of existing standards for water quality and human consumption; [and] consideration of dissolved oxygen . . . to determine whether the Alberta-Pacific proposal can proceed and meet the governments' aquatic standards. (Review Board Report: Recommendations 9.4.1, 9.4.2, pp. 89-90)

The studies were to take into consideration the cumulative impacts of effluent from all the pulp mills on the Peace-Athabasca river system. Review Board members estimated it would take three to five years for the studies to be done properly.

The Review Board made several other equally important recommendations, including improvements in the EIA process; public review of the forest management agreement following negotiation and consultation with native people, and prior to approval of the mill; and a comprehensive review of the site selected in comparison to more remote locations.[6]

The findings of the Review Board represented a significant victory for community groups and environmentalists; however, the provincial government and the company were still determined to go ahead with the project without delay. According to Paul Edwards, who reviewed the Alpac EIA process for the Environmental Law Centre:

Alpac was granted a private audience with [Premier] Getty and three other members of his government. Following this meeting, Mr. Getty remarked publicly that the Review Board had failed to assess critically the information provided at the public hearings.[7]

In his public comments on the Review Board Report, Getty alleged that:

This board was like a mirror. . . . It just took everything that came and put it all into the report, and therefore it was really incumbent that you'd better have a balance of input because that was the only way you could have a balance coming out again. And that didn't happen.[8]

Not only did Getty express the opinion that the Review Board's report was unbalanced, he disclosed that Alberta-Pacific, the spurned suitor, had told his government there were errors in the report. The Province of Alberta responded to Alpac's claim by commissioning a "review of the review." The Finnish pulp and paper research consulting firm Jaakko Pöyry was hired to conduct an independent assessment of the scientific data that had been presented to the Review Board. Getty said that this scientific review was "going to tell us if all the facts were accurate. . . . Alpac themselves say that they feel there are some errors in assessment. And we think we owe it to them to go through that technical assessment." The Premier also reckoned that he couldn't abandon northern Alberta communities. "We have to make sure that we do what's right and balanced and not get caught up in emotions or the environmental groundswell, because sustainable development is possible."[9] Paul Edwards noted in his review that "this was an unusual step, as a review board's report is generally intended to be the last step in an EIA . . . prior to a final decision."[10]

Defending the Review Board's recommendations as being based on scientific principles "any idiot could understand," Review Board member David Schindler declared, "It's obvious the government wants to do everything it possibly can to make this development go ahead. They seem to confuse scientific evidence with some sort of popularity contest."[11] Unfortunately for the government, Jaakko Pöyry's findings, released in June 1990, were consistent with those of the Review Board.[12]

In response to the Review Board's report, in July 1990, the provincial and federal governments announced a $10 million three-year study of the Peace, Athabasca, and Slave rivers. The governments thus gave the appearance of following a Review Board recommendation, while rejecting, without mention, the Board's further recommendation that the mill not proceed until the study was complete.[13]

In the meantime, Alpac had presented the Alberta government with a plan for a process change, titled *Mitigative Response to Concerns Regarding Chlorinated Organic Compounds*.[14] One of the changes proposed was eliminating the use of molecular chlorine in the bleaching process, and substituting 100 per cent chlorine dioxide. The report of the Scientific Review Panel cited Alpac as claiming that the changes it proposed would drastically reduce the production of organochlorines, from up to 1.3 kilograms per air-dried tonne of pulp in the process originally proposed, to less than 0.25 kilograms per air-dried tonne in the new process.[15] The Alberta government commissioned a Scientific Review Panel composed of three members, chosen from the federal and provincial civil services, to study the feasibility of Alpac's mitigative process. In September 1990, the Panel held a hearing in Athabasca.

This chapter explains how the government and Alpac circumvented the Alpac EIA Review Board's recommendations—how politics triumphed over the public and the scientific findings that had been aired, debated, and clarified in the Alpac EIA hearings. We look at four questions raised by members of the public about the Scientific Review: Why was the environmental review narrowed to a technical assessment? Why was good science considered less relevant than industrial design? Why should the public trust the track record of the pulp-mill industry? and Can science address moral questions?

From Environmental Review to Technical Assessment

> The Terms of Reference of the Review Panel shall be to inquire into and advise the Minister of the Environment on the improvements proposed by Alberta-Pacific Forest Industries Inc. to the wood-pulping and bleaching process as they relate to the mitigation of the discharge of chlorinated organics into the Athabasca River. (Scientific Review: Appendix 1)

> The Panel . . . attempted to define expected rates of organochlorine discharge at specified levels of confidence. The Panel did not attempt to determine whether these expected organochlorine discharge rates were acceptable.

Such considerations clearly fall outside of the Panel's Terms of Reference. (Scientific Review: 8)

Clearly, there is a scientific gap between the report of the original EIA Review Board and your mandate. Who will place and assess your report in the context of the March 2, 1990, Alpac EIA Review Board report? (Merilyn Peruniak, Scientific Workshop: 748-749)[16]

The "Mitigative Response" submitted by Alpac was released for public scrutiny prior to the hearing, and written assessments of the document were requested by the Panel. Some environmental groups were given intervenor funding to hire counter-experts to assess the document. Public participation was restricted—material scheduled for presentation at the hearing had to have been approved in advance by the Scientific Review Panel. The hearing was not called a "public hearing," but a "scientific workshop" on technical issues. Some members of the public thought they were being short-changed:

At the previous set of hearings there was 500 people attended, 750 submissions presented, none refused, at 11 locations. I think it almost makes a bit of a mockery of this one. I'm embarrassed for you on that. . . . There are no Natives here. At the last one there were. They came all the way from the Northwest Territories, and they came indeed with their scientific experts. The Government of the Northwest Territories came, and they are on record as saying they are not coming to these ones because the Terms of Reference are too narrow. (Jim Darwish, Scientific Workshop: 800-801)

The terms of reference of the Scientific Review Panel were significantly narrower than those of the EIA Review Board (see the opening quotation for this section), and the Panel chose to interpret them even more narrowly than necessary:

Our interpretation that we have placed on [the terms of reference] is that we are talking about mitigation in terms of the [wood-pulping and bleaching] process and the process only. We do not believe that we have the mandate to consider environmental effects, and therefore do not propose to be considering them. (E. R. Brushett, Scientific Review Panel chairman, Scientific Workshop: 15)

Alpac proposed in its "Mitigative Response" to use technologies and a bleaching process which it had told the EIA Review Board only three months previously were either not feasible or technically unproven. Recalling this earlier evaluation of the technology, EIA Review Board member David Schindler offered this assessment of the "Mitigative Response" and the mandate and composition of the Scientific Review Panel:

[M]itigation measures are supposed to alleviate some of the Board's stated concerns regarding organochlorine contamination. Some of these involve techniques which our Board was told were not practical. There are a number of environmental consequences of the proposed technology that will not be significantly alleviated, and some new environmental problems. While I am submitting a review to the mitigation board, I note that the board does not include either ecologists or toxicologists, and that the terms of reference are so narrow as to make it questionable whether environmental considerations will even be considered.[17]

In fact environmental concerns, including those raised by Schindler, were explicitly excluded from the review. The Panel recorded that many submissions focused erroneously "on the impacts on the environment of any effluent or emission, which are issues beyond the Terms of Reference," and complained that even the federal Department of Fisheries and Oceans (DFO) had mistakenly interpreted the terms of reference to mean "the Review Panel will consider the effectiveness of the proposed mitigation measures in reducing potential impacts on fish and fish habitat."[18] The Panel did not revise its interpretation of its mandate, despite arguments from DFO that Alpac had not substantiated its claims with respect to mitigation of possible adverse impacts on fish and fish habitat.[19] Thus, the government and the Panel transformed an ecosystem issue into an engineering question by isolating the pulp production process from the receiving environment of the Athabasca River.[20] The Panel washed its hands of Merilyn Peruniak's concern that there was "a scientific gap" between the Panel's mandate and the report of the EIA Review Board. The public's worst fears about the governments' disregard for the findings of the EIA Review Board were coming true.

Science versus Industrial Design

> Although the Panel was appointed to do a "scientific" review, it rejected science in favour of "an evolving empirical understanding of applied industrial design" (Section 2.2 pages 8 and 9). Such principles of good science as confirming results, replicating trials, testing assumptions and hypotheses, and the desirability of reaching conclusions that would stand up to peer review are all rejected. (Bill Fuller)[21]

> Industrial designers do not need to fully understand why a process functions. They must however, be confident that it will function. Although such confidence can be aided by a good understanding of the underlying physics and chemistry, real confidence can only come from the successful implementation of an industrial design. Therefore, industrial designers rely more on industrial scale empirical evidence, than on rigorous scientific analysis of the underlying process fundamentals. (Scientific Review: 9)

The evidence in support of Alpac's "Mitigative Response" was of poor quality. Much of the information presented by Alpac came from manufacturers of equipment the company proposed to purchase. Alpac also drew conclusions based on unsubstantiated results reported by other mills, personal communications and observations, confidential reports, or in-house trials in which no indication of experimental conditions was given. In one instance, the authors of the "Mitigative Response" claimed that the Daishowa pulp mill in Peace River would provide evidence of the technical feasibility of the proposed Alpac process. At this time, however, Daishowa was still under construction, and had yet not begun operating.[22]

Neil McCubbin, an engineering consultant commissioned by the Scientific Review Panel to assess Alpac's revised pulping process, defended the use of industry-generated evidence. McCubbin explained that while "data . . . published at leading scientific conferences and journals subject to peer review are generally accepted as being more credible than information from private and/or unidentified sources," he felt that "it is currently impractical to analyze a proposal on state-of-the-art technology purely on the basis of publications." He explained that pulping technologies are changing rapidly to meet market pressures for reduced organo-chlorine emissions, and that competition in the pulp industry breeds a need for secrecy that forces industry scientists to delay publishing until months after a technology has been subjected to trials or experimental runs. McCubbin concluded, "I have had to rely to a greater extent than I would have liked on telephone conversations and access to private documents of clients in forming the opinions expressed in this document."[23]

A number of the studies that Alpac cited were publications or presentations by the Pulp and Paper Research Institute of Canada (PAPRICAN), whose major sponsor is the Canadian Pulp and Paper Association "which is basically the member companies, the mills . . . producing pulp and paper in Canada."[24]

While PAPRICAN does some original research, it also acts as "a broker for information" from mills around the world.[25] It was learned at the workshop that Environment Canada also supports PAPRICAN, and that the federal government contracted PAPRICAN to assess Alpac's mitigative proposal. Thus, the federal government had asked PAPRICAN, a primarily industry-sponsored research institute, to advise it on a proposal that drew heavily on PAPRICAN and pulp industry research.[26]

In the previous hearing, the public and the Review Board had used the standard of good science to question the impact science presented by Alpac. In the scientific workshop, calls for good science were rejected by Richard Berry, who presented PAPRICAN's assessment, and by Douglas Reeve, an expert advisor to the Scientific Review Panel. For example, as the discussion on the first day of the workshop revealed, results of tests had been presented in the "Mitigative Response" with no indication of how they were arrived at—no indication of how many trials had been done, or what the experimental conditions were. Both Berry and Reeve publicly expressed trust in Alpac's mitigative process, yet when asked whether they had seen the experimental data on which the results were based, both said they had not:

John McInnis (Official Opposition environment critic): [D]id you ask for the mill trials from Alpac or Kamyr, the mill trials referred to today?

Berry: No. (Scientific Workshop: 143)

McInnis: In the Alpac submission the reference for the data on AOX coming out of this process is . . . not formally footnoted in the document. Were you given access to those trials?

Reeve: No, I was not given access to those trials.

McInnis: Don't you think that's a fairly crucial piece of evidence?

Reeve: Yes, I think it is a crucial piece of evidence. (Scientific Workshop: 45-46.)

Some members of the public raised questions about Berry's and Reeve's willingness to support Alpac's claims without having access to the data supporting those claims:

McInnis: Why did you not ask for the Kamyr-Alpac mill trials? . . . Even though it was cited as evidence in the mitigation proposal?

Berry: I looked at the literature that I had available to me and I concluded that, yes, that was reasonable. So I didn't need to see the trials to determine whether or not I agreed with it. . . . All I was judging was a figure, and I had to determine whether that figure was appropriate. (Scientific Workshop: 144)

Mitch Bronaugh (Friends of the North, Edmonton branch): Alpac's claim for their AOX discharge level is based on one thing, that one thing you have not had access to, you don't know what's in it. Your statement that you believe the process will work, it seems to me very difficult to understand that this could have any scientific basis.

Reeve: [A] lot of industrial design is not entirely based on science, it is based on experience, because sometimes science cannot adequately describe how the process works. . . . If you ask me, has this been scientifically demonstrated that it will function according to strict rules of scientific evidence, the answer is no. (Scientific Workshop: 49, 51)

Jim Darwish, another member of the Edmonton branch of Friends of the North, characterized the results of allowing industrial design to precede scientific proof:

Dr. Reeve, during his discussion on the first day, pointed out that in the pulp and paper industry, science often follows the industry, that innovations are introduced, and then science catches up to it. That was my understanding of the thrust of what he said. . . . He put his finger on the problem that exists in the pulp mill industry and why they alone account for over 60 per cent of all the pollution in Canada. . . . The reason is . . . that government[s] have allowed industry to tinker and tamper and experiment with our rivers and lakes and forests and air. And the result is the pollution of the rivers and lakes. (Scientific Workshop: 804-805)

Scientific Workshop or Revival Meeting?

Mitch Bronaugh: When you responded . . . you said, yes, I believe it will work. Of course when you say "I believe" something, I think of religion rather than science.

Douglas Reeve: A scientist working on industrial problems cannot limit himself to science alone. Scientists like myself operating on industrial processes . . . have to learn from the experience. . . . That's where I have my religion, if you like, my belief that this will function. (Scientific Workshop: 44, 50-51)

Was faith in industrial reports and industrial experience justified? Having established that the Scientific Review Panel and its consultants had not seen the data for the bleaching trial on which

Alpac based its claim to be able to reduce organochlorines in its emissions, members of the public insisted that the data be presented for assessment. A special evening session was convened for presentation of the data. When Alpac showed up without the intention of distributing copies of their data, the public insisted that the chair delay the session until duplicates were made for the Panel and the audience. The session was eventually adjourned until the next morning, because intervenors objected that the data Alpac had finally presented was uninterpreted—no indication was given of the relationship between the raw data and results reported in the mitigative document.

The next morning, it became evident that Alpac's prediction about the total organochlorines to be produced by its new fibre line was based on a single measurement from one laboratory simulation of the bleaching process. The scale and nature of that laboratory test were described by Ed Becker and Mike Holloran, employees of the companies that had performed the test:

> Becker: The cooking was carried out on 10 kilograms oven-dry weight of chips and a 2-cubic-foot digester. The other stages [washing and bleaching] were carried out on approximately 300 grams oven-dry of pulp. (Scientific Workshop: 277)

> Malcolm Wilson (Panel member): Is this one analytical result of one sample?

> Holloran: Yes.

> Wilson: So there's no averages in here or anything like that?

> Holloran: This is a one-time analysis of this sample. (Scientific Workshop: 292)

James Plambeck, an analytical chemist at the University of Alberta who was hired as a counter-expert by the Edmonton branch of Friends of the North, explained to the Scientific Review Panel that it was not an acceptable scientific practice to base a number in a scientific report on a single measurement from a single test run. It is well known that measurements taken of a single sample or of samples from different test runs of the same experiment will vary, and it is important to determine by how much. This variance will determine how confident one can be about one's results. Science students are taught about variance and confidence levels in first- or second-year university courses, or even earlier. Plambeck explained the point this way:

> I would like to start explaining . . . by quoting to you from our current elementary textbook of chemistry, *Quantitative Chemical Analysis*, by D. C. Harris . . . about analytical chemistry and the law. "Analytical chemists must always emphasize to the public that the single most important characteristic of any result obtained from one or more analytical measurements is an adequate statement of its uncertainty interval."

> There isn't an uncertainty interval given in the Alpac report. What is worse, with respect to AOX, the discussion which is truly relevant to the question of whether or not this mill should be built is that number. That number is a single measurement on a single sample, never repeated. It has no standard deviation. Mr. Chairman, in my field, it has no credence. (Scientific Workshop: 337)

Exasperated and very concerned, Plambeck offered the Panel these conclusions about pulp and paper industry data:

> A scientist who writes a report of any sort may be forgiven by his peers for a wrong interpretation of his data. . . . What he will not be forgiven for is an absence of data. He will not be forgiven for data which is not clearly documented. He will not be forgiven for data when you can't tell what was done. That's outside the ground rules of science.

> I have come closer to encountering data outside the ground rules of science here than at any other controversy I've ever had the misfortune to step into. Gentlemen, if this is the situation of the pulp and paper industry, I can only echo the command of the gentleman as heard on high, may God help us all. (Scientific Workshop: 817-818)

Plambeck's interventions helped the public to understand that rejecting the call for good science meant rejecting the requirement to present evidence to back up claims. In its Report, the Scientific Review Panel agreed with Plambeck that Alpac's figure for organochlorine production, on its own, was "not credible." However, the Panel compared Alpac's figure with other data available to it. Most of these data derived from unpublished reports and were admitted to be unreliable because they were reported without uncertainty intervals. The Panel then concluded, on the basis of this evidence, that the Alpac figure was reliable, "Most of the data points are of less than ideal reliability individually. . . . Nevertheless, they show a reasonably linear trend."[27] Bill Fuller, retired zoologist and member of the Friends of the Athabasca, responded, "I am . . . mystified by the scientific process that transforms data of 'less than ideal reliability individually' into data that can be relied on en masse!"[28]

At the scientific workshop, following Plambeck's presentation, Mitch Bronaugh again expressed the opinion that the testimony presented by industry experts and advisors had more in common with religion than with science, "[T]hey have said it will work on the basis of their experience. . . . This is not scientific testimony. It is a series of testimonials more like in a camp meeting or a religious revival."[29]

Tammy Warawa, an environmentalist, took Bronaugh's point one step further, asking why the public should rely on the testimony of industry experts and advisors, given the track record of the pulp-mill industry:

> [H]ere we are being told, no, we don't have any . . . tests that will prove this will work. We're supposed to rely on your . . . judgment. And it's been rather awful in the past. . . . You do not have a good track record, and I'm seriously concerned that we have to take your word for it. (Scientific Workshop: 811-812)

A Giant Laboratory

> Would you . . . suggest that it would be to the advantage of all of us to wait three years until we know as much about the river as possible before we commit ourselves to primarily

an experimental technology that has never been tested?
Would you say that that would be good, common sense or
scientific sense? (Peter Opryshko, Scientific Workshop: 238)

Mill-site resident Opryshko posed this question to Margaret-Ann
Armour, a chemistry professor at the University of Alberta, who had
spoken at the invitation of the Scientific Review Panel. Her
presentation on chlorine dioxide substitution supported Alpac's
claim that dioxin would be virtually eliminated in the new process.
Opryshko felt that Armour "had walked blindly into a controversy,"
"added her weight to the other side at the eleventh hour," and "was
legitimating a hearing process that was clearly biased and that was
not science." When Opryshko asked Armour whether she supported
the recommendation of the Alpac EIA Review Board that river
studies be conducted prior to approval of the mill, he "was
challenging her ethics because her science was going to be used for
something that all kinds of scientists had said no to." Opryshko
believed that "scientists should be responsible not only for their
research, but how their research will be used in a controversy."[30]

Armour: You asked the question, in three years will we know
more than we know now? In three years you could ask the
same question and get the same answer. We never are going
to know everything. We are hearing more and more about
risk. We have to balance risk against what we know the risk is
going to do, and we have to do that at all times. We can't
continually postpone things.

Opryshko: Agreed, but you are aware the previous panel
suggested—and it was done very logically—first of all,
[studies] about whatever the state of the river is; look
carefully at the FMA . . . a closer evaluation or proper site
selection . . . Now, I am not suggesting a forever moratorium.
I am suggesting sort of a parallel: let the company keep
developing their technology, and let them run their pulping
tests for three more years before we commit to
construction. Would that not be the common-sense way to
proceed before we allow them to get into the ground and
then we can't go back? Would that not be the common
sense or scientific way to do it?

Armour: That's very much a call of judgement. And I have heard so often people say, let's wait, we will get the answer after another three years. Three years have passed, and we are not any closer to the answer than before. . . . There are many instances in science where people have kept saying let's do some more studies, and the studies have raised more questions than they have answered. There has to come a time where you say, okay, we will or we won't. (Scientific Workshop: 239-240)

Armour's answers implied that she believed the risks of building the mill were not great enough to justify a delay while river studies were done, especially since "we are never going to know everything." Her use of the word "everything" was misleading. It is true that scientists will never know everything—they can establish only probabilities, not certainties. The real question becomes, what should we do when faced with scientific uncertainty, and who should make decisions in the face of uncertainty and risk.

Opryshko: I live in the community where this thing is going to be created. Would you suggest that we should sacrifice our home to a giant lab?

Armour: Oh, I would love it if you would do that because I would come and work in the lab.

Opryshko: Well, you agree, then, with the Alpac manage-ment, and their owners and masters in Japan, that that's what they would love to do. And you would love to do it too, so thank you. (Scientific Workshop: 239-241)

Opryshko's cynicism was fuelled by his interpretation of Armour's position on risk—that it was time to "take a chance" with industrial sized beakers, with little regard for people's health and community.

There was little discussion of the limits of science and how to deal with uncertainty either in the Alpac EIA hearings or in the Scientific Workshop. The only scientist who explicitly recognized the ethical and moral issues embedded in debates about pollution impacts was Jack Vallentyne, who spoke at the Alpac EIA Review

Board hearings. By implication, Vallentyne recognized that decisions on risk should be made by the whole community, not just by scientists:

> The general rule is that governments ban chemicals on a one-by-one basis only when "proof" of adverse effects is found. In the opinion of the Science Advisory Board,[31] this reactive behaviour is unwise, unscientific and immoral. . . . Reactive behaviour in relation to toxic chemicals is considered to be immoral because: it impinges on the rights of humans; on the rights of future generations; and on the rights of other species to freedom from environmental insult. The use or non-use of toxic chemicals is not a question that science can resolve. Because it is primarily a moral question, its resolution will not wait for all the facts to come in. (Edmonton: 4913, 4917)

The call for "studies first" went down to defeat. In October 1990 the Scientific Review Panel concluded that Alpac's new process was feasible.[32] On December 21, 1990, Premier Getty entered a packed hall in Athabasca to announce approval of the Alpac mill. Bill Fuller was not impressed: "I have no words strong enough for politicians who misuse science and scientists in an effort to legitimate dubious decisions."[33] Mitch Bronaugh offered this description of the scientific review:

> I suppose maybe this could be called "political" science. We find a lot of this "political" science when a lot of money is at stake. Right now we have a billion dollars at stake in this pulp mill and more than that in profits, and I don't know how much in personal expectations from various politicians. (Scientific Workshop: 229)

And, in the Alberta Legislature, Official Opposition environment critic John McInnis characterized the government's position:

> [T]hey took the politically and legally dangerous course of setting aside an environmental assessment and substituting their own judgment. With the rationale of this three-member panel, we have three men and a minister who override the rest of the world.[34]

Notes

1. *The Alberta Government Presentation on the Report of the EIA Review Board on The Proposed Alberta-Pacific Pulp Mill,* Athabasca Community Centre, Athabasca, Alberta, March 2, 1990, p. 3.
2. *Alberta-Pacific EIA Review Board Report/Public Meeting,* Athabasca Community Centre, Athabasca, Alberta, March 2, 1990, p. 16.
3. The Alberta Government Presentation on the Report of the EIA Review Board, p. 11.
4. Alberta-Pacific EIA Review Board Report/Public Meeting, p. 11.
5. This and all further citations of the Review Board Report in this chapter refer to Alberta-Pacific Environmental Impact Assessment Review Board, *The Proposed Alberta-Pacific Pulp Mill: Report of the EIA Review Board, March 1990* (Edmonton, Alberta: Alberta Environment, 1990). Quotation from the Executive Summary.
6. Review Board Report, Recommendations 9.4.4, 9.4.5, 9.4.6, pp. 90-91.
7. Paul Edwards, "The Alberta Pacific Pulp Mill Proposal: A Review of the Environmental Assessment of a Bleached Kraft Pulp Mill," *Journal of Pesticide Reform* 10, no. 2 (Summer 1990): 14-17. Quotation from p. 16.
8. "Getty Slams Pulp Panel for Unbalanced Report," *The Edmonton Journal,* March 24, 1990.
9. *Ibid.*
10. Paul Edwards, p. 16.
11. "Scientist Stood Up to the Premier," *The Edmonton Journal,* April 8, 1990.
12. See Jaakko Pöyry, *Complementary Scientific Review of the Alberta-Pacific Pulp Mill Project* (Helsinki, Finland: Jaakko Pöyry Oy) June 15, 1990; and W. A. Fuller, "Critique of the Jaakko Pöyry Report," *The FOTA Files: Pulp Mill Pollution and Politics 1988-1991* (Athabasca, Alberta: Friends of the Athabasca Environmental Association, 1991), pp. 89-102.
13. Canada-Alberta News Release No. 76, July 12, 1990. See also, W. A. Fuller, "Smoke and Mirrors: How to Misinform with Half Truths," *The FOTA Files: Pulp Mill Pollution and Politics 1988-1991* (Athabasca, Alberta: Friends of the Athabasca Environmental Association, 1991), pp. 75-78.
14. Alberta-Pacific Forest Industries Inc., *Mitigative Response to Concerns Regarding Chlorinated Organic Compounds* (Edmonton, Alberta: Alberta-Pacific Forest Industries Inc.) July, 1990.
15. This and all subsequent citations of the Scientific Review in this chapter refer to The Alberta-Pacific Scientific Review Panel, *A Review of the Modified Wood Pulping and Bleaching Processes Proposed for Alberta-Pacific Forest Industries Inc. Pulp Mill* (Edmonton, Alberta: Alberta Environment) 1990. This information is contained in the Executive Summary.
16. Quotations from the Scientific Workshop from *J.G. Moore and Associates Ltd., Alberta-Pacific Scientific Review Panel, Volumes 1-6* (Edmonton, Alberta: J.G. Moore and Associates Ltd.) 1990.

17. Letter from David Schindler to federal environment minister Robert de Cotret. David Schindler, Alberta-Pacific Scientific Review Panel Submission #5 August 21, 1990. Attachment K, p. 2.

18. Scientific Review: 6.

19. See Department of Fisheries and Oceans, Alberta-Pacific Scientific Review Panel Submission #10 August 23, 1990. David Schindler's review of the mitigative response contained a similar criticism: "Alpac would in any case still contribute significantly to the organochlorine inputs to the river. If Alpac's figure of 0.25 kg/ADT can be achieved, the total loading of AOX to the Athabasca River in 1993 will still be 60% of 1987 values . . . The small size of the river renders almost any input of AOX questionable." Alberta-Pacific Scientific Review Panel Submission #5 August 21, 1990, pp. 3-4.

20. James Lovelock calls the separation of a technology from its broader implications, such as occurred here, "scientific apartheid." See *The Ages of Gaia: A Biography of Our Living Earth* (New York: Bantam Books, 1990), pp. 11, 61.

21. W. A. Fuller, "Critique of the Report of the Scientific Review Panel," *The FOTA Files: Pulp Mill Pollution and Politics 1988-1991* (Athabasca, Alberta: Friends of the Athabasca Environmental Association, 1991), p. 116.

22. Often, in the "Mitigative Response," evidence of even the stand-alone technical performance of components proposed for combination in the Alpac fibre line was based on "personal communications and observations" [Reference #63]; "unpublished presentations" by or to Alpac consultants [References #43, #46, #48, #49 and #62]; "unpublished studies" by Alpac's consultants [Reference #83]; or conclusions drawn from bleaching trials, reported without description or explanation, by Alpac's technical supplier [the Kamyr-Alpac bleaching "trials," see note, bottom of Table 5.5, "Mitigative Response," p. 111]. Combinations of this evidence were then presented as if to suggest these were the equivalent of proven industrial performance trials. See also "Mitigative Response," page 72, for reference to evidence from a mill which had not yet begun operations.

23. Neil McCubbin, Alberta-Pacific Scientific Review Panel Submission #21, pp. 2-3.

24. Richard Berry, Scientific Workshop: 55, 56.

25. Richard Berry, Scientific Workshop: 119.

26. For PAPRICAN papers and presentations cited by Alpac in its "Mitigative Response," see footnotes 43 and 51. For discussion of the circular assessment process used by the federal government, see Scientific Workshop: 118-119. Dr. Reeve, the technical consultant to the scientific panel, works for the Pulp and Paper Centre at the University of Toronto, which is funded 50 per cent by the pulp and paper industry. (Scientific Workshop: 43-44)

27. Scientific Review: 34.

28. W. A. Fuller, "Critique of the Report of the Scientific Review Panel," p. 123.

29. Scientific Workshop: 819.

30. Follow-up interview with hearings presenter Peter Opryshko, Athabasca. July 1993.

31. Jack Vallentyne is the Chairman of the Canadian section of the International Joint Commission's Great Lakes Science Advisory Board.

32. Scientific Review: Executive Summary.

33. W. A. Fuller, "Critique of the Report of the Scientific Review Panel," p. 116.

34. *Alberta Hansard,* 22nd Legislature, 3d Session, no. 8 (March 21, 1991): 130. John McInnis, MLA Edmonton Jasper Place and Official Opposition environment critic, question to Alberta Minister of Environment.

**Environment Minister Ralph Klein at the press conference to announce
approval of the Alpac pulp mill**
(Photograph courtesy of *The Athabaskan*)

Conclusion: The Value of Public Participation

The [hearing] increased the public's awareness of the issue enormously . . . it attracts media attention and it brings information out to the people, and it gives a platform to people who might not have a platform. . . . [A]nd the result of that happening, the public . . . hears different points of view. Industry, government are challenged publicly, they have to respond publicly, so their attitudes are modified through that process, too. . . . [I]f it was a perfect world their [EIA Review Board] recommendations would be also viewed as important, and acted upon. But that didn't happen. (Dennis Bevington)[1]

Although there was some disappointment that the government didn't follow strictly [the EIA Review Board recommendations], still it was worth it, for me personally, to get involved and dig into these areas. It was a time of personal growth, developing a certain amount of expertise which I hope to continue. . . . I got involved in environmental concerns and became known in the community as a person who is concerned about that, earned a certain amount of respect. (Arnold Labrentz)[2]

Given the outcome described in Chapter 8, was participating in the Alpac EIA public hearings a wasted effort for public participants opposed to the mill, or worse, did public involvement help legitimate a questionable decision? Should the public refuse to participate in environmental public hearings?

Dennis Bevington and Arnold Labrentz maintain that the hearings were beneficial, even though the Alberta government rejected the recommendations of its own EIA Review Board. Bevington, the Mayor of Fort Smith, feels that the hearings increased public awareness and provided for a public airing of issues. Labrentz talks about his personal growth and involvement in environmental concerns.

Throughout the book, you have read how members of the public used the hearings to criticize the EIA and public hearing processes; to raise questions about the Alberta government's contradictory roles in attracting and financing international pulp and paper firms, and then reviewing their environmental suitability; to question cosy working relationships among industry consultants and members of public review agencies; and to deplore the fact that transnational corporations were taking financial support from the Alberta government while exporting value-added jobs overseas and leaving pollution in Canada. Intervenors also forced public disclosure of a number of industry studies, and compelled representatives of the provincial and federal governments to table relevant information from studies about the current state of the Peace-Athabasca river system. Finally, public pressure led Alpac to make many changes to the design and operation of its mill, in addition to the elimination of elemental chlorine from the bleaching process. Refusing to participate in public hearings, even those as flawed as the Alpac hearings, would mean forfeiting such gains. It would also mean failing to recognize that the hearings were only one step in the long process of public scrutiny that will be required over Alpac's twenty-year life-span.

However, EIA public hearings, as they are presently constituted in Alberta, are seriously flawed. Their findings are not binding on the government, and they face internal restrictions, such as narrowness of mandate. Most importantly, the hearings are held too late in the process of making decisions about resource use. Jack Van Camp puts the point this way:

> The environmental assessment process overall, I'm kind of ambivalent about the whole thing . . . it's got real limitations as far as coming up with optimum solutions . . . they're very reactive . . . [and] may help us get rid of bad proposals. I think it is much more important now to come up with good proposals to really take the momentum away from bad proposal writers.[3]

The "good proposals" Van Camp talks about should build on publicly reviewed conservation and resource use plans, and publicly reviewed intergovernmental agreements on the use of inter-boundary waters, jurisdiction over resources such as forests, and minimum standards of environmental protection, such as levels of dissolved oxygen in rivers.

Equally importantly, good proposals and a fair EIA hearing process require public involvement to begin long before projects reach the public hearing stage:

> Consultation should occur before a project gets an approval in principle . . . both industry and government should have involved our community long before any decisions were made, what industry was contemplated, what technology was to be used, what was the size of the development, what companies were involved and where the location of any project would occur. (Peter Opryshko, Prosperity: 7450-7452)[4]

Even with these improvements, however, hearings may still prove inhospitable to the public. This book began with Harry Garfinkle speaking highly of environmental public hearings as a "mandatory adjunct of the democratic process of informed decision-making." He was optimistic that the Alpac hearings would provide citizens the "opportunity to stand up and speak out," assist "minority groups to have their positions brought into the public domain," and protect against "the tyranny of the majority." What Garfinkle talked about did happen, but the freedom to speak out would have been mere window-dressing had public participants not challenged the constraints of the hearing process, and the authority and language of company-paid experts.

Challenging Expert Opinion

> I think with this process, you have been launched into the next decade; the 1990s, when people will be listened to. The little hunter, the little trapper, the little people on the land are the ones that are going to be making decisions for people that will use our natural resources. I think this is what you have launched with a process that's very unique. It doesn't exist too much across Canada where the considerations of a province, Northwest Territories, and the national values are examined under a microscope like this. (Cindy Gilday, Review Board member, Prosperity: 7628-7629)

There are some basic evidentiary rules when you are dealing with complex scientific issues. In the courts, these sorts of issues are traditionally resolved on the basis of expert opinion. . . . I am not saying that the large range of opinion from individuals and companies and organizations should be totally ignored. . . . The important thing was that people be heard . . . but I don't think that a lot of it necessarily plays a major part in your [Review Board] final decision. (Dennis Thomas, lawyer for Alpac, Prosperity: 7586, 7587, 7589)

In the closing session of the Alpac hearings, Cindy Gilday expressed an optimistic view of future environmental public hearings, in which people on the land would make decisions about resource use. She was obviously impressed by the hundreds of hours of presentations by ordinary people. At the same session, Alpac's lawyer, Dennis Thomas, tried to counter the effect of those hours of testimony by saying that the Review Board should listen to experts and discount the testimony of non-experts. It is worth fighting to ensure that Thomas' view does not prevail. However, given the ruling government's failure to implement the Alpac EIA Review Board's recommendations, and the acquiescence of the federal and provincial environment ministries, it is unlikely that Gilday's view of the hearing process will be realized in the near future.

Traditionally, government and industry scientists and technical experts have provided the data for decisions by EIA review boards. To weaken the hold of these experts, public participants at the Alpac EIA hearings revealed divisions in expert opinion by enlisting the assistance of counter-experts, believing that the best weapon against Alpac's scientists was another scientist. The counter-experts typically presented evidence that contradicted Alpac's claims, or argued that Alpac's science lacked the qualities of good science—data to back up conclusions, replication of experimental trials, statements of uncertainty, and peer reviewed sources of data and information. Many of their presentations undermined the professional hegemony of Alpac's scientists. Once division in expert opinion was revealed, more consideration was given to alternative understandings of mill impacts presented by non-specialists.

For example, lay members of the public established that specialists had made measurements and calculations based on faulty assumptions about their localities, thus poorly estimating the true impacts of the mill on these communities. They also protested that Alpac's EIA addressed impacts in isolation, and asked the Review Board to consider cumulative and synergistic effects of two or more impacts. Native people argued that the science in the EIA failed to recognize traditional knowledge. And some scientists and lay people showed that Alpac's technical discussions of pollution failed to take into account special populations at risk and the necessity of ethical decision making in the face of uncertainty. Such criticisms were more effective than a simple denunciation of science as ideology would have been.

Social context also played a role in the attempt to weaken the hold of technical experts. It was fortunate, for example, that the Alpac EIA Review Board held hearings in downstream communities, because residents of these communities placed the discussion of environmental impacts and even scientific studies in a cultural and economic context different from that portrayed by the company and mill boosters. Participants from these communities argued convincingly that they could experience negative effects from the mill, yet would reap no benefit from it.

Debates led by non-specialists and counter-experts at the Alpac hearings suggest promising new emphases in environmental impact assessment, such as basing assessment on the holistic approach of ecology, and integrating traditional native knowledge and local knowledge of communities with western science. Recognition and discussion of uncertainty at all stages of measurement, modeling, and prediction are important as well. Learning to identify and debate ethical and moral issues embedded in risk assessment and environmental decision-making are perhaps the most crucial. Together, these new directions should diminish the dominant role of scientists and experts and allow for greater involvement of non-scientists in environmental decision-making.

Participation after All

If you are wondering whether participation is worth the effort, consider the inequality of power among the groups facing each other at the Alpac hearings. Relatively uninformed, unorganized individuals in rural northern communities found themselves up against the money and influence of transnational corporations, the authority of specialists and experts, and a provincial government that had already approved the mill in principle. Yet public intervention was so effective that Alpac could not persuade the Review Board to approve the mill. The provincial government could not even buy Alpac a reversal of the decision with the Jaakko Pöyry review. In order to push through the mill, the Alberta government had to create a kangaroo court which was not allowed to consider the effects of the "mitigative" process on the environment. Thus, the government's political decision could no longer be masked by the hearing process and dressed up in such phrases as "environmental integrity," "sustainable development," or "ecologically sound." The public denied Alpac and the Alberta government claim to these words.

Our Alpac case study concerns only one small part of one environmental controversy. Confrontation over environmental issues continues in Athabasca, and many other places. It is clear that public participation in the Alpac public hearings did make a difference. However, participation in public hearings is not enough. Sustained political activity is required beyond the hearing process.

Notes

1. Follow-up interview with hearings presenter Dennis Bevington, Fort Smith, NWT. September, 1992.
2. Follow-up interview with hearings presenter Arnold Labrentz, Fort Smith, NWT. September 1992.
3. Follow-up interview with hearings presenter Jack Van Camp, Fort Smith, NWT. September 1992.
4. All items identified as "Filed Documents" are written submissions to the Alpac EIA Review Board, a collection of the Filed Documents is housed in the Athabasca University Library; quotations from the Alberta-Pacific EIA Review Board public hearings are from J. G. Moore and Associates Ltd., *The Alberta-Pacific Environment Impact Assessment Review Board Public Hearing Proceedings, Volumes 1-55* (Edmonton, Alberta: J. G. Moore and Associates Ltd., 1989).

Bibliography

Adkin, Laurie E. "Counter-hegemony and Environmental Politics in Canada." In *Organizing Dissent: Contemporary Social Movements in Theory and Practice,* edited by William K. Carroll, pp. 135-156. Toronto: Garamond Press, 1992.

Alberta-Pacific Environmental Impact Assessment Review Board. *The Proposed Alberta-Pacific Pulp Mill: Report of the EIA Review Board, March 1990.* Edmonton, Alberta: Alberta Environment, 1990.

Alberta-Pacific Forest Industries Inc. *Alberta Pacific Forest Industries Inc. Environmental Impact Assessment. Bleached Kraft Mill Public Participation Program.* Edmonton, Alberta: Alberta-Pacific Forest Industries Inc., 1989.

Alberta-Pacific Forest Industries Inc. *Alberta-Pacific Forest Industries Inc. Environmental Impact Assessment. Supplemental Information.* Edmonton, Alberta: Alberta-Pacific Forest Industries Inc., 1989.

Alberta-Pacific Forest Industries Inc. *Alberta-Pacific Forest Industries Inc. Written Submissions and Responses Volumes 1, 2 and 3.* Edmonton: Alberta-Pacific Forest Industries Inc., 1989.

Alberta-Pacific Forest Industries Inc. *Mitigative Response to Concerns Regarding Chlorinated Organic Compounds.* Edmonton, Alberta: Alberta-Pacific Forest Industries Inc., 1990.

Alberta-Pacific Forest Industries Inc., *Alberta-Pacific Forest Industries Inc. Environmental Impact Assessment. Bleached Kraft Pulp Mill Main Report.* Edmonton, Alberta: Alberta-Pacific Forest Industries Inc., 1989.

Alberta-Pacific Scientific Review Panel. *A Review of the Modified Wood Pulping and Bleaching Processes Proposed for Alberta-Pacific Forest Industries Inc. Pulp Mill.* Edmonton, Alberta: Alberta Environment, 1990.

Andersen, Roger. *The Power and the Word: Language, Power and Change.* London: Paladin Grafton Books, 1988.

Aronowitz, Stanley. *Science as Power: Discourse and Ideology in Modern Society.* Minneapolis: University of Minnesota Press, 1988.

Ashforth, Adam. "Reckoning Schemes of Legitimation: On Commissions of Inquiry as Power/Knowledge Forms." *Journal of Historical Sociology* 3, no. 1 (March 1990): 1-22.

Barnes, Barry. *About Science.* Oxford: Blackwell, 1985.

Berger, Mr. Justice Thomas. *Northern Frontier, Northern Homeland: The Report of the Mackenzie Valley Pipeline Inquiry.* Ottawa: Supply and Services Canada, 1977.

Bourdieu, Pierre. *Language and Symbolic Power,* edited and with an introduction by John B. Thompson, translated by Gino Raymond and Matthew Adamson. Cambridge: Polity Press, 1991.

Brown, Donald A. "The Most Important Problem for Environmental Ethics: The Failure to Integrate Environmental Ethics into Daily Environmental Decision Making." In International Forum for Biophilosophy, *Stability and Change in Nature: Ecological And Cultural Dimensions,* Proceedings of the IFB Conference, Budapest, Hungary, March 1992.

Brunk, Conrad, Lawrence Haworth, and Brenda Lee. *Value Assumptions in Risk Assessment: A Case Study of the Alachlor Controversy.* Waterloo, Ontario: Wilfrid Laurier University Press, 1991.

Campbell, Jessica. "Forum File: Index on Pulp and Paper Pollution." *Canadian Forum* (June-July 1991): 32.

Caroll, William K., ed. *Organizing Dissent: Contemporary Social Movements in Theory and Practice.* Toronto: Garamond Press, 1992.

Clow, Michael, Aloysius Hayes, and Peter MacDonald. "Contrasting Paths of Development in Tree Harvesting Systems on the Miramichi." Paper delivered at the Canadian Political Science Association, Political Economy Section, Learned Societies Annual Meeting, Charlottetown, PEI, June 4, 1992.

Cover, Lynn. "Solving the Paradox of Public Participation in Environmental Planning: Evaluation of an Alberta Case Study." Major paper for Masters Diss., York University, 1992.

Daly, Herman E., and John B. Cobb, Jr. *For the Common Good: Redirecting the Economy Toward Community, the Environment and a Sustainable Future.* Boston: Beacon Press, 1989.

Davies, Natalie Zemon. *Society and Culture in Early Modern France.* Stanford: Stanford University Press, 1975.

Doern, G. Bruce, and Peter Aucoin, eds. *The Structures of Policymaking in Canada.* Toronto: MacMillan, 1971.

Dunk, Thomas W., ed. *Social Relations in Resource Hinterlands.* Thunder Bay, Ontario: Lakehead University Centre for Northern Studies, 1991.

Dunk, Thomas. "Talking About Trees: Images of the Environment and Society in Forest Workers' Discourse." Paper delivered at the sessions on Sociology and the Environment, at the CSAA Annual meetings, Charlottetown, PEI, June 1992.

Edwards, Paul. "The Alberta Pacific Pulp Mill Proposal: A Review of the Environmental Assessment of a Bleached Kraft Pulp Mill." *Journal of Pesticide Reform* 10, no. 2 (Summer 1990): 14-17.

Edwards, Paul. *The Al-Pac Review Hearings: A Case Study.* Edmonton, Alberta: The Environmental Law Centre, 1990.

Forester, John, ed. *Critical Theory and Public Life.* Cambridge: Massachusetts Institute of Technology Press, 1985.

Foucault, Michel. "The Subject and Power." *Critical Inquiry* 8 (Summer 1982): 777-795.

Freeman, Milton R. "The Nature and Utility of Traditional Ecological Knowledge." *Northern Perspectives* 20, no. 1 (Summer 1992): 9-12.

Friends of the Athabasca Environmental Association. *The FOTA Files: Pulp Mill Pollution and Politics 1988-1991.* Athabasca, Alberta: Friends of the Athabasca Environmental Association, 1991.

Fuller, W. A. "Critique of the Jaakko Pöyry Report." In *The FOTA Files: Pulp Mill Pollution and Politics 1988-1991,* pp. 89-102. Athabasca, Alberta: Friends of the Athabasca Environmental Association, 1991.

Fuller, W. A. "Critique of the Report of the Scientific Review Panel." In *The FOTA Files: Pulp Mill Pollution and Politics 1988-1991,* pp. 115-126. Athabasca, Alberta: Friends of the Athabasca Environmental Association, 1991.

Fuller, W. A. "Facing the Future—An Environmentalist's Perspective." In *Sustainable Use of Canada's Forests: Are We on the Right Path,* edited by Kim Sanderson, pp. 13-16. Edmonton, Alberta: Canadian Association of Environmental Biologists, 1991.

Fuller, W. A. "Smoke and Mirrors: How to Misinform with Half Truths." In *The FOTA Files: Pulp Mill Pollution and Politics 1988-1991,* pp. 75-78. Athabasca, Alberta: Friends of the Athabasca Environmental Association, 1991.

Fuller, W. A., Michael Gismondi, and Mary Richardson. "Ethnocentrism in Scientific Standards." In International Forum for Biophilosophy, *Stability and Change in Nature: Ecological And Cultural Dimensions,* Proceedings of the IFB Conference, Budapest, Hungary, March 1992.

Gilbert, G. Nigel, and Michael Mulkay. *Opening Pandora's Box: A Sociological Analysis of Scientists' Discourse.* Cambridge: Cambridge University Press, 1984.

Gismondi, Michael, and Mary Richardson. "Discourse and Power in Environmental Politics: Public Hearings on a Bleached Kraft Pulp Mill in Alberta, Canada." *Capitalism Nature Socialism* 2, no. 8 (October 1991): 43-66.

Gordon, Anita, and David Suzuki. *It's a Matter of Survival.* Toronto: Stoddard, 1990.

Government of Alberta, Department of Forestry, Lands and Wildlife. "Proactive Government is Successful." *Programs, Activities and Initiatives.* Edmonton, Alberta: Alberta Forestry, Lands and Wildlife, 1990.

Government of Alberta, Department of Forestry, Lands and Wildlife. *Alberta Forest Development Opportunities.* Edmonton, Alberta: Alberta Forestry, Lands and Wildlife, 1989.

Government of Alberta, Department of Forestry, Lands and Wildlife. *Major Forestry Projects.* Information Package for Departmental Staff for Public Involvement Sessions February-April 1989. Edmonton, Alberta: Alberta Forestry, Lands and Wildlife, 1989.

Government of Alberta. *The Alberta Government Presentation on the Report of the EIA Review Board on The Proposed Alberta-Pacific Pulp Mill, Athabasca Community Centre, Athabasca, Alberta, March 2, 1990.* Edmonton, Alberta: Government of Alberta, 1990.

Government of Canada, Environment Canada. *Aquatic Toxicity of Pulp and Paper Mill Effluent: A Review.* Ottawa: Supply and Services Canada, 1987.

Government of Canada, Environment Canada. *A Report on Canada's Progress Towards a National Set of Environmental Indicators,* SOE Report No. 91-1. Ottawa: Supply and Services Canada, 1991.

Harrison, Kathyrn. "Federalism, Environmental Protection, and Blame Avoidance." · Paper delivered at the Canadian Political Science Association Annual Meeting, Kingston, Ontario, 1991.

Hirschkop, Ken. "Bakhtin, Discourse and Democracy." *New Left Review* 160 (November-December 1986): 92-113.

Hutchinson, Roger. *Prophets, Pastors, and Public Choices: Canadian Churches and the Mackenzie Valley Pipeline Debate.* Waterloo, Ontario: Wilfrid Laurier University Press, 1992.

International Forum for Biophilosophy. *Stability and Change in Nature: Ecological And Cultural Dimensions,* Proceedings of the IFB Conference, Budapest, Hungary, March 1992.

Jaakko Pöyry, *Complementary Scientific Review of the Proposed Alberta-Pacific Pulp Mill Project Environmental Impact Assessment.* Helsinki, Finland: Jaakko Pöyry, Oy., 1990.

Jacobs, Peter, and Barry Sadler. *Sustainable Development and Environmental Assessment: Perspectives on Planning for a Common Future.* Ottawa: Canadian Environmental Assessment Research Council, 1991.

Johnson, Martha. "Dene Traditional Knowledge." *Northern Perspectives* 20, no. 1 (Summer 1992): 3-5.

Johnstone, Barry, and Michael Gismondi. "A Forestry Boom in Alberta?" *Probe Post* 12, no. 1 (Spring 1989): 16-19.

Kemp, Ray. "Planning, Public Hearings and the Politics of Discourse." In *Critical Theory and Public Life,* edited by John Forester, pp. 177-201. Cambridge: Massachusetts Institute of Technology Press, 1985.

Killingsworth, M. Jimmie, and Dean Steffens. "Effectiveness in the Environmental Impact Statement: A Study in Public Rhetoric." *Written Communication* 6, no. 2 (1989): 159.

Lather, Patti. *Feminist Research in Education: Within/Against.* Geelong, Victoria, Australia: Deakin University, 1991.

Latour, Bruno. *Science in Action: How to Follow Scientists and Engineers through Society.* Cambridge: Harvard University Press, 1987.

Levy, Edwin. "The Swedish Studies of Pesticides and Cancer." In *Environmental Ethics,* edited by Raymond Bradley and Stephen Duguid, pp. 187-200. Burnaby, BC: Institute for the Humanities, Simon Fraser University, 1989.

Lincoln, Bruce. *Discourse and the Construction of Society: Comparative Studies of Myth, Ritual, and Classification.* New York: Oxford University Press, 1989.

Lovelock, James. *The Ages of Gaia: A Biography of Our Living Earth.* New York: Bantam Books, 1990.

McDonald, Michael. "Ethics versus Expertise: The Politics of Technology." In *Ethics and Technology: Ethical Choices in the Age of Pervasive Technology,* edited by Jorge Nef, Jokelee Vanderkop, and Henry Wiseman, pp. 119-124. Toronto: Wall and Thompson, 1989.

Moore, J. G., and Associates Ltd. *The Alberta-Pacific Environment Impact Assessment Review Board Public Hearing Proceedings, Volumes 1-55.* Edmonton, Alberta: J. G. Moore and Associates Ltd., 1989.

Moore, J. G., and Associates Ltd. *Alberta-Pacific Scientific Review Panel, Transcripts, Volumes 1-6.* Edmonton, Alberta: J.G. Moore and Associates Ltd., 1990.

Nakashima, Douglas J. *Application of Native Knowledge in EIA: Inuit, Eiders and Hudson Bay Oil.* Ottawa: Supply and Services Canada, 1990.

Nef, Jorge, Jokelee Vanderkop, and Henry Wiseman, eds. *Ethics and Technology: Ethical Choices in the Age of Pervasive Technology.* Toronto: Wall and Thompson, 1989.

Nikiforuk, Andrew, and Ed Struzik. "The Great Forest Sell-off." *Toronto Globe and Mail, Report on Business Magazine* 6, no. 5 (November 1989): 57-68.

Novek, Joel, and Karen Kampen. "Sustainable or Unsustainable Development? An Analysis of an Environmental Controversy." *Canadian Journal of Sociology* 17, no. 3: 249-273.

Palmer, Bryan. *Descent into Discourse: The Reification of Language and the Writing of Social History.* Philadelphia: Temple University Press, 1990.

Parenteau, R. *Public Participation in Environmental Decision-making.* Hull, Quebec: Federal Government Assessment Review Office, 1988.

Proctor, Robert N. *Value Free Science?: Purity and Power in Modern Knowledge.* Cambridge: Harvard University Press, 1991.

Rees, William. "Sustainable Development and the Biosphere: Concepts and Principles." Paper presented to Teilhard Studies, 1990.

Resnick, Philip. "State and Civil Society: The Limits of a Royal Commission." *Canadian Journal of Political Science* 20, no. 2 (June 1987): 379-401.

Rohleder, F. "Cause of Death in Workers Exposed to Dioxins at BASF, Ludwigshafen, Germany, in 1953." Paper delivered at the 9th International Symposium of Chlorinated Dioxins and Related Compounds, Toronto, Ontario, 17-22 September, 1989.

Roots, E. F. "Some Concepts and Issues Surrounding the Place of Science in Assessment of Impacts on the Environment." Presentation for the Workshop on the Role of Science in Environmental Impact Assessment, Edmonton, April, 1992.

Rowe, J. Stanley. "The Effects of Pulp Mills on the Environment." Paper delivered at the Workshop on Bleached Kraft Pulp Mill Technology and Environmental Issues, Athabasca, Alberta, 1 March 1989.

Rutkowsky, Jim, and Joel Russ. "Forests, Water and Public 'Participation'." *The New Catalyst* no. 23 (Spring 1992): 4-5.

Salter, Liora. *Mandated Science: Science and Scientists in the Making of Standards*. Dordrecht, Holland: Kluwer Academic Publishers, 1988.

Salter, Liora, and Debra Slaco. *Public Inquiries in Canada*. Ottawa: Supply and Services Canada, 1981.

Sanderson, Kim, ed., *Sustainable Use of Canada's Forests: Are We on the Right Path?* Edmonton, Alberta: Canadian Society of Environmental Biologists, 1991.

Schindler, David. "A Critique of Proposed Federal Regulations for Pulp and Paper Effluent and Recent Evidence Implicating Dioxins as Hazards to Human Health." Unpublished manuscript, 1991.

Schrecker, Ted. "Ethics and Institutions: How We Think About Policy Decisions." In *Environmental Ethics*, edited by Raymond Bradley and Stephen Duguid, pp. 207-215. Burnaby, BC: Institute for the Humanities, Simon Fraser University, 1989.

Scott, James C. *Domination and the Arts of Resistance*. New Haven: Yale University Press, 1990.

Seabrook, Jeremy. *The Myth of the Market: Promises and Illusions*. Montreal: Black Rose Press, 1991.

Sherman, Joan, and Michael Gismondi. "Community Environmental Indicators: A Case Study of the Alpac EIA Hearings." Unpublished report. 1992.

Study Group on Environmental Assessment Hearing Procedures. *Public Review: Neither Judicial, Nor Political, But an Essential Forum for the Future of the Environment*. A Report Concerning the Reform of Public Hearing Procedures for Federal Environmental Assessment Reviews. Ottawa: Supply and Services Canada, 1988.

Taylor, J. D. *Environmental Health Issues Associated with A Modern Bleached Kraft Pulp Mill*. Edmonton, Alberta: Alberta-Pacific Forest Industries Inc., 1989.

Tester, Frank. "Reflections on Tin Wis: Environmentalism and the Evolution of Citizen Participation in Canada." *Alternatives: Perspectives on Society, Technology and Environment* 19, no. 1 (October 1992): 34-41.

Valverde, Mariana. "As if Subjects Existed: Analysing Social Discourses." *Canadian Review of Sociology and Anthropology* 28, no. 2 (1991): 173-187.

Voss, R. H. "Trace Organic Contaminants in Pulp and Paper Mill Effluents and Their Environmental Effects." *Pulp and Paper Research Institute of Canada, Miscellaneous Reports*, No. 112.

Wein, E. E. "Nutrient Intakes and Use of Country Foods by Native Canadians near Wood Buffalo National Park." Ph.D. Diss., University of Guelph, 1989.

Willis, P., and P. Corrigan. "Orders of Experience: The Differences of Working-class Cultural Forms." *Social Text* 7 (Spring-Summer 1983): 85-103.

Wilson, V. Seymour. "The Role of Royal Commissions and Task Forces." In *The Structures of Policy-making in Canada*, edited by G. Bruce Doern and Peter Aucoin, pp.113-129. Toronto: MacMillan, 1971.

World Commission on Environment and Development. *Our Common Future*. Oxford: Oxford University Press, 1987.

Wynne, Brian. *Rationality and Ritual: The Windscale Inquiry and Nuclear Decisions in Britain*. Chalfont St. Giles, England: The British Society for the History of Science, 1982.

Index

List of Acronyms

Alpac	Alberta-Pacific Forest Industries Inc.
AOX	adsorbable organic halides
API	American Paper Institute
ATC	Athabasca Tribal Council
BC	British Columbia
CLI	Canada Land Inventory
CPU	Canadian Paperworkers Union
DFO	Department of Fisheries and Oceans
DOE	Department of the Environment
EARP	Environmental Assessment and Review Process
ERCB	Energy Resources Conservation Board
FMA	Forest Management Area
FOTA	Friends of the Athabasca Environmental Association
GNP	Gross National Product
IFB	International Forum for Biophilosophy
IQ	intelligence quotient
kg/ADT	kilograms per air-dried tonne
LC50	lethal concentration at 50 per cent
MLA	Member of the Legislative Assembly
NWT	Northwest Territories
PAPRICAN	Pulp and Paper Research Institute of Canada
PCB	polychlorinated biphenyl
PEI	Prince Edward Island
RCMP	Royal Canadian Mounted Police
SO_2	sulphur dioxide
SOE	state of the environment
2378-TCDD	tetrachlorodibenzo-p-dioxin
2378-TCDF	tetrachlorodibenzo-furan

Index